T0294529

COME, STAY, LEARN, PLAY

American Alliance of Museums

The American Alliance of Museums has been bringing museums together since 1906, helping to develop standards and best practices, gathering and sharing knowledge, and providing advocacy on issues of concern to the entire museum community. Representing more than 35,000 individual museum professionals and volunteers, institutions, and corporate partners serving the museum field, the Alliance stands for the broad scope of the museum community.

The American Alliance of Museums' mission is to champion museums and nurture excellence in partnership with its members and allies.

Books published by AAM further the Alliance's mission to make standards and best practices for the broad museum community widely available.

COME, STAY, LEARN, PLAY
A Guide to Making the Museum Experience

Andrea Gallagher Nalls

ROWMAN & LITTLEFIELD
Lanham • Boulder • New York • London

Published by Rowman & Littlefield
An imprint of The Rowman & Littlefield Publishing Group, Inc.
4501 Forbes Boulevard, Suite 200, Lanham, Maryland 20706
www.rowman.com

6 Tinworth Street, London SE11 5AL, United Kingdom

British Library Cataloguing in Publication Information Available

Library of Congress Cataloging-in-Publication Data

Names: Nalls, Andrea Gallagher, author. | American Alliance of Museums.
Title: Come, stay, learn, play : a guide to making the museum experience / Andrea Gallagher Nalls.
Description: Lanham : Rowman & Littlefield, [2021] | Includes bibliographical references and index.
Identifiers: LCCN 2021018665 (print) | LCCN 2021018666 (ebook) | ISBN 9781538146620 (cloth) | ISBN 9781538146637 (paperback) | ISBN 9781538146644 (ebook)
Subjects: LCSH: Museums—Management. | Museum visitors. | Museums—Social aspects. | Museums—Educational aspects.
Classification: LCC AM121 .N35 2021 (print) | LCC AM121 (ebook) | DDC 069/.1—dc23
LC record available at https://lccn.loc.gov/2021018665
LC ebook record available at https://lccn.loc.gov/2021018666

For Sean, Cam, and Andie.

With enormous thanks to C. J. Roberts, Maria Steijlen, Lisa Richardson, Manny Leto, Malerie Dorman, Rodney and Krissy Kite-Powell, Nicole Conner, Brad Massey, Julie Matus, Susan Rimensnyder, Colleen Fernandez, Mr. Tom Touchton, and the staff of the Tampa Bay History Center. I am grateful to have learned from you.

In appreciation of the tremendous patience held by my editors, Charles Harmon and Erinn Slanina.

And lastly, to my entire visitor services family, it's you who makes the museum experience magic.

Contents

Foreword, by Nicole Krom   ix

Introduction   1

1 Visitor Experience Staff   7
2 A Whole-Museum Commitment to Service   29
3 Experience Staff as DEAI Advocates   43
4 The Experience Economy Approach, Applied in a
   Museum Setting   55
5 Magnetic Modeling and Dynamic Delivery: The Business
   of Museums   65
6 Onetime Visitors to Lifelong Friends   79
7 The Curators of Experience   89
8 Post-Disaster Museum Experience   103
9 On Making the Museum Experience   113

Appendix   Making the Museum Experience: Self-Assessment   117

Index   121

About the Author   126

Foreword

IN THIS TIME OF CONSTANT CHANGE, forced nimbleness, and quick response, I can only think of how those in visitor-facing roles have been demonstrating these traits for decades. We have been forced to reimagine our day-to-day tasks, experiences, services, and operations in a variety of ways during the 2020 pandemic—but in reality, it's nothing new for those working with visitors. Our niche has a long history of adjusting plans and elevating them to meet everyday realities. When constantly faced with the unexpected, visitor experience staff find ways to mold unpredictable situations into meaningful experiences with grace, humor, and professionalism.

In the past decade, the importance of visitor experience has heightened and been shown more understanding at all levels of institutions. After all, what are museums without visitors and their staff? They'd cease being museums and become beautiful storage buildings. So, we challenge everyone who is passionate about cultural institutions to continue to recognize and promote the importance of the visitor experience in their own circles. To continue to model that quality service, combined with meaningful and attentive engagement, leads to exceptional experiences for visitors and staff. Those exceptional services can lead to healthier work cultures, visitor satisfaction, and revenue. This work must be inclusive and people-first. Institutions are nothing without the people whose work propels and upholds the mission.

Throughout this book, we hope you engage (or re-engage) with the importance of this work and the larger museum field, especially in these challenging times. We hope you continue to display grace, humor, and professionalism—and to break barriers. Visitor experience should be the fundamental priority of any cultural organization, and I am excited about the future of you and this incredible community.

Nicole Krom
Founder and Chairperson, Visitor Experience Group;
Membership and Outreach Manager,
Longwood Gardens in Kennett Square, Pennsylvania

Introduction

I N 2011, PETER SHANKMAN, an author and entrepreneur, boarded a flight to Newark after a long day of back-to-back meetings. Shankman had left his home in New Jersey at 3:30 a.m. that morning to catch a 7 a.m. flight and was now returning on the 5 p.m.

Just before take-off, Shankman realized that he hadn't eaten since lunch and he wouldn't be able to eat until after the flight landed, so he jokingly tweeted:

> Hey @Mortons—can you meet me at Newark airport with a porterhouse when I land in two hours? K, thanks.[1]

He then shut his phone off for the two-and-a-half-hour flight back home.

When Shankman arrived in Newark, he was surprised to find a tuxedoed man holding a bag. The man, named Alex, was from Morton's The Steakhouse in Hackensack, New Jersey, which was about twenty-four miles away from the airport. Alex went on to give Shankman a 24 oz. porterhouse and an order of shrimp, potatoes, bread, and, of course, silverware.

We live in a time where a person's experience with an organization or brand dictates whether or not that organization or brand obtains customer loyalty and affection. These days, everyone is a discerning experience critic. With online evaluation platforms like TripAdvisor and Yelp, it's easy to whip out your phone and either notate or even take a picture of the experience, good or bad, and share it in real-time with everyone you know.

A good experience at your museum comes down to this same idea of producing world-class moments and letting those moments be a motivating factor for your visitor to return. Consider this: Who would you trust more? An advertisement or a reliable friend telling you what a fantastic time they had somewhere? Shankman's experience with Morton's The Steakhouse has been shared countless times. It's one of those apocryphal stories to which organizations aspire.

A person can get a steak at countless restaurants, but it's the experience that will keep them brand-loyal; likewise, museums can be siloed and stuffy with a "no-touch" policy or they can be warm and welcoming places of comfort.

In 2011, a woman in North Carolina lost the diamond from her wedding ring while trying on clothes at a Nordstrom store. A store security worker saw her crawling on the sales floor under the racks. Once he realized what she was looking for, he joined the search.[2]

They couldn't locate the stone, so the employee asked two building-services workers for help. They opened up the store's vacuum cleaner bags, where they found the diamond from the ring. It was neither the ingenuity of Nordstrom's marketing department that elevated the woman's experience from terrible to terrific that day, nor was it the strategic brilliance of Nordstrom's top executives; it was the genuine care and concern of the security officer and facilities staff—all frontline, front-of-house employees—that created this experience. This is a classic example of their "Nordstrom Way," a customer service culture so revered it's studied as a model and hinges on their salespeople putting themselves in the shoes of their customers.[3]

I first became interested in making the museum experience twelve years ago as a frontline museum staff person. I recognized that no matter how robust our collection or high-quality our programming was, we as a museum would fail without successful delivery. Museums have the opportunity to inspire, educate, and bring people together, but in a moment—with just one small negative interaction—that possibility can be threatened.

Research by the American Alliance of Museums (AAM) has shown that museums are essential. As economic engines, museums support more than 726,000 American jobs and contribute $50 billion to the US economy each year. They are anchors of community and quality of life. More people visited an art museum, science center, historic house/site, zoo, or aquarium in 2018 than attended a professional sporting event. As digital educators, museums receive millions of online visits to their websites each year from diverse online communities, including teachers, parents, and students (also including those who are home-schooled). From a social service perspective, museums provide programs for children on the autism spectrum, English as a Second Language classes, and programs for adults with Alzheimer's or other cognitive impairments. From a formal education standpoint, museums spend more than $2 billion each year on education activities; the typical museum devotes three-quarters of its education budget to K–12 students and receives approximately fifty-five million visits each year from students in school groups. Children who visited a museum during kindergarten had higher achievement scores in reading, mathematics, and science in third grade than children who did not. Children who are most at risk for deficits and delays in achievement also see this benefit.

Museums are committed to ensuring that people of all backgrounds have access to high-quality experiences in their institutions. In 2012, 37 percent of museums were free or had suggested admission fees only; nearly all others offered discounts or free admission days. Since 2014, more than five hundred museums nationwide have facilitated more than two and a half million museum visits for low-income Americans through the Museums for All program. About 26 percent of museums are located in rural areas; other museums reach these communities with traveling vans, portable exhibits, and robust online resources.

And from a public-trust perspective, the American public considers museums the most trustworthy source of information in America, rated higher than local papers, nonprofit researchers, the US government, and academic researchers. Museums preserve and protect more than a billion objects. Museums are considered a more reliable source of historical information than books, teachers, or even personal accounts by relatives.

Ninety-seven percent of Americans believe that museums are educational assets for their communities, and 89 percent believe that museums contribute essential economic benefits to their community.[4]

Museums add value to people's lives, and as the people running those museums, we have a responsibility to be sharply focused on how to make museum-goers happy, how to teach them, how to make our museums safe and welcoming places for them, and how to make them want to come back.

I was reminded of the passion and tenacity of museum frontline employees when I realized that those I was interviewing (on ways they created successful museum experiences) were all monumentally talented and could have taken their sharp minds and excellent ideas to a different sector, where they might have (actually, definitely would have) made more money. Many came from an education, marketing, or curatorial background, but they made a promise to themselves and the museum field somewhere along their career trajectory. They committed their talents to the success of museums by dedicating their expertise to museum experience.

In 2019, I submitted a session proposal to the AAM to speak at that year's annual conference in New Orleans, Louisiana, on converting onetime visitors into lifelong friends. What began as an inquest into why people would want to come back more than once to a museum, turned into a realization that it was through positive interactions with museum workers that visitors were most likely to form a bond. So, we presented ways to connect with visitors to create lasting memorable moments and win their favor. The response from the Alliance audience was overwhelmingly positive. In a standing-room-only session, we talked about how building personal relationships builds organizational success.

When the decision was made to write this book, I turned to that audience, and others like them—those talented, dedicated, frontline museum people who are committed to endearing their guests. As a result of these conversations, fantastic ideas emerged, and a more specific definition of "museum experience" was refined:

> The museum experience is the emotion or reaction a visitor feels due to the organization's efforts during visitor/museum interaction.

To be a successful museum experience professional, you must harbor sincere love for your institution and your mission, because that devotion is what will propel you to do better, even on the most challenging days. Making a museum experience isn't simple, and it's not for the faint of heart. But it is possible. And in this text, we will explore how.

This book is divided into various experience tracks such as hiring and training the right experience curators, breaking down silos, the importance of diversity, accessibility, inclusion, and equality for visitor comfort, visitor-to-member conversion, and visitor engagement—among other topics that will show you how to support a positive museum experience.

You will find that there is much reference to for-profit organizations. This is not to suggest cultural institutions have the resources that for-profits do—quite the contrary, actually—but synthesizing research conducted within the for-profit sector is advantageous to us for that exact reason. Museums do not have the resources that many for-profits do, so let's allow them to hire the consultants, have entire departments conjure up new and exciting experience ideas, and spend the time and money fine-tuning what makes for an excellent experience. Then, let's learn from them.

By the end of our time together, I am hopeful you will find that making museum experience requires the prioritization of people—staff and visitors—over all else within a museum; yes, that even includes the exhibits and collection. It was not always true, but today, most museums exist to attract and serve visitors.[5] Especially in today's world.

The consumer marketplace has recently been through a catastrophic time, fraught with uncertainty and stress. We need museums to re-form our sense of community and to reassure us that what's always been, will continue to be. The COVID-19 pandemic upended the way we all live. There is a requisite yearning for comfort, familiarity, consistency, and—honestly—distraction now more than ever.

Good museums serve their visitors well, and their front-line museum staff have an incredible opportunity to affect that success. Let's unpack how.

Notes

1. Conradt, Stacy. "11 Of the Best Customer Service Stories Ever." *Mental Floss*, December 15, 2015. https://www.mentalfloss.com/article/30198/11-best-customer-service-stories-ever.

2. Martinez, Amy. "Tale of Lost Diamond Adds Glitter to Nordstrom's Customer Service." *Seattle Times*, May 11, 2011. https://www.seattletimes.com/business/tale-of-lost-diamond-adds-glitter-to-nordstroms-customer-service/.

3. Spector, Robert. *The Nordstrom Way*, second edition. Hoboken, NJ: John Wiley & Sons, 2012.

4. "Museum Facts & Data." *About Museums*, American Alliance of Museums (website), August 10, 2020. https://www.aam-us.org/programs/about-museums/museum-facts-data/.

5. Falk, John H. *Identity and the Museum Visitor Experience*. New York: Routledge, 2016.

1

Visitor Experience Staff

To make our understanding of what it takes to have a positive visitor experience within a museum more useful, we must start with the people who have the ability to shape that experience. The principal reason for this chapter is to establish a vision of what a successful visitor experience staff looks like for your organization. These baseline ideas can be the foundation of the creation of your own visitor experience philosophy, which will define where you want to take your visitor experience team and how you plan to get them there. This chapter deals with qualities to look for and traits to draw out from frontline personnel, the demographic and psychological makeup of a powerful visitor experience team, and training strategies to support the ability to provide quality interactions. Key elements include

- answering, what is a visitor experience professional?;
- prioritizing the museum experience;
- personalizing the approach;
- acknowledging the importance of human interaction;
- traits of a visitor experience star;
- making the museum experience magical;
- leaving egos at the door;
- the value of strong leadership;
- recognizing that each member of the team is essential;
- the significance of diversity; and
- the need for balance and support.

These ideas focus specifically on visitor experience staff and are threaded throughout other chapters, but right now we will focus on finding and training the right people—forming the right team—to accomplish what all museum visitors want: a positive experience.

What Makes a Visitor Experience Professional?

Museums serve many purposes. And people visit museums with different motivations.

Museums, like many other cultural attractions, are essentially experiential products, quite literally constructions to enable experience. In this sense, museums are about facilitating feelings and knowledge based on the personal observation or contact of their visitors.[1]

One of the most directly correlated influences on a positive perception of a museum visit is the exchange a visitor has with its staff. Recognizing there are types of experience other than social—such as object experience, cognitive experience, and introspective experience—this chapter deals with the social aspect as shaped by museum frontline staff.

How a visitor feels upon engagement with a component of a museum will be dependent on the preset biases and past experiences one enters with. The only thing that will change a perception is the non-static, or fluid, interactions—the experience of that visitor with the museum's staff, and those interactions will be different every single time.

What sets visitor experience professionals apart from the rest of the museum staff? The visitor experience staff has a primary focus of making sure each visitor wants to come back. In many departments within a museum, the staff may never see the community it serves. The opposite is so for visitor experience staff, who are primarily frontline staff at a museum but could be anyone. As soon as any museum staff person steps into a public area, he or she becomes a part of the visitor experience.

Prioritize the Museum Experience

Museum engagement is the ability to occupy the attention or efforts of a visitor. Museum experience is the process of personally observing, encountering, or undergoing something at a museum. So, the ability to engage is almost entirely dependent on the experience. Joseph Pine II and James Gilmore's *The Experience Economy*[2] produces a nebulous notion that goods and services are no longer enough, people seek experiences. The term "experience economy" began with a few simple ideas in the late 1990s—escapism, education, entertainment, and esthetic—but it has recently been expanded to include personalization, communities, localness, hospitableness, serendipity, and ethical consumerism, according to a *Boston Hospitality Review* article on the notion.[3]

FIGURE 1.1
We've moved into the experience economy.
Source: Adapted from Pine and Gilmore (2014).[4]

No property or platform can deliver all of these things. In fact, the goal is to set up the guest to have these experiences—a serendipitous moment, for instance—rather than to hand-deliver the experiences to the guest. To become a conduit for experiences, museums must acknowledge that the foundation of its experience is its hospitality. "Hospitality" is not a word most connect with museums. Hospitality rests on the hospitable nature of people. A museum that is both experience-driven and customer-centric becomes "experiencentric." An experiencentric museum can be found at the intersection of intellectual and emotional connection and interpersonal contact.

Personalize Your Approach

Most museums have a mission statement. They may even have vision and values statements, too. Mission statements have the ability to provide insight and direction to an institution. Take the mission statement for your institution and examine how the persons interacting with your guests can support your mission. For example, if your museum's mission is, "To serve and inspire our community, and to increase the awareness of modern art within," then your guest experience mission statement might be, "To exceed the service needs of our visitors and find what will inspire them." Just as a mission statement can guide a museum, an experience statement (most effectively a sub-statement of your mission that explains what frontline service staff plan to do to carry out the mission) can guide your experience philosophy and make it into a measurable, obtainable overarching goal to work toward. It also provides a standard.

Standards are helpful to prevent staff from feeling that they don't know or understand what is expected of them. Creating an experience statement can provide a framework to lessen any confusion and set a standard within which to work.

Your experience statement should be unique. All museums are different, and that is what makes the diverse museum community effective. Every frontline approach will be fluid. Where your museum is right now is very different from where your museum will be in two, five, ten, and twenty years. And that's good! That change keeps your institution relevant and constantly examining what is working for your team.

In the *New Gold Standard: 5 Leadership Principles for Creating a Legendary Customer Experience Courtesy of the Ritz-Carlton Hotel Company*,[5] the Ritz Carlton Hotel Company relies on three fundamental "Steps of Service":

1. A warm and sincere greeting. Use the guest's name.
2. Anticipation and fulfillment of each guest's needs.
3. Fond farewell. Give a warm goodbye and use the guest's name.

These three steps of service are intended to simplify the approach to interactions with the *New Gold Standard*'s approach to guests. It is a fundamental yet incredibly effective tool to ensure each guest feels cared about, which is the desired outcome. By weaving these three steps into their interactions, the guest walks away feeling cared for.

Factors in Customization of Approach

Fluidity in a museum's experience approach is dependent on characteristics of that museum. Some characteristics of a museum that will affect the customization of its experience philosophy are:

- content/theme
- audience
- geographic location
- age of institution
- staffing limitations

Of course, there are other variables as well. The experience philosophy of a children's museum will necessarily be vastly different than that of a contemporary sculpture museum. They will both be centered on providing great service but will differ in their details and application. If you know you have a high concentration of French-speaking visitors, then you may want to ensure someone on staff is fluent, or even teach frontline associates light French phrases or have some kind of translator tool handy at the desk. If you know families with small children comprise a good percentage of your visitation, your visitor services professionals should be versed in all of the camps, programs, and gallery enhancements your museum offers for younger kids. Tailor the experience so that it's appropriate for your audience based on the summary of your institution's characteristics. For most organizations, the ability to adapt a service experience is the responsibility of frontline employees, but is a function of management setting expectations and allocating appropriate resources. Visitor services managers need to train on how and when to adapt a visitor's service experience. A study done by the *Journal of Service Research* on tailoring to visitors' needs[6] identifies two major processes in adapting a service experience: (1) recognition of visitor needs through employee empathy and anticipation and (2) creation of alternatives to meet those needs through employee creativity. The study indicated that perceived service climate has a larger impact on recognition of customer needs, while empowerment has a stronger influence on the creation of alternatives. This research highlights that for the best outcomes adaptive behavior can, and should, be taught to anyone interacting with museum visitors.

Acknowledge the Importance of Human Interaction

There is no substitute for human interaction, especially when the digital and the static elements complement one another. Cognitive computing, machine learning, virtual reality, and artificial intelligence are all buzzwords we have come to know. As the world experiences a shift to a mechanized, computer-programmed version of its former self, the museum industry also feels those effects.

A computer can do many things—extensive computations within seconds, teach someone how to make a roux, give live updates on sports scores—the list of what a computer is capable of is endless.

Customer service interactions are on a spectrum with two axes: emotion and urgency. Each mode of customer service has its own space on that quadrant.

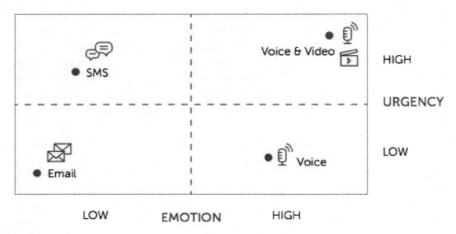

FIGURE 1.2
The four quadrants of customer service delivery.
Source: Paiva 2017.[7]

As figure 1.2 shows, one thing a computer cannot do well is make someone feel like they are of primary importance. A smile, a kind and compassionate tone of voice, and a genuine willingness to help are elements that a computer cannot effectively impart.

A study conducted by *Forbes* on the possibility of artificial intelligence (AI) replacing humans in the customer service industry[8] found that new AI tools are rapidly emerging in the support space that can address high-urgency situations, but when it comes to high-emotion scenarios, no AI can replicate human empathy, so there's still a distinct advantage to having a real person help a visitor.

Visitor experience professionals can do this. They can be the reason people want to return. Computers cannot build relationships in the way actual people can build relationships.

What to Look for in a Visitor Experience Professional

Traits of an exemplary frontline experience person include:

- a welcoming presence
- a genuine desire to interact
- a concierge-type approach to any need

And their philosophy is: "Do unto your customers as you want to be treated when you're a customer." Almost everyone possesses the fundamental ability to be nice. It's the golden rule, to treat others the way you'd like to be treated. The key is to break down the barriers that individuals face when trying to keep the golden rule at the forefront.

It's easy to determine what traits are desirable in order to have an experiencentric approach, but how do you teach your people those traits? You encourage them to be nice. Being nice to one another and nice to your guests is, at its core, an exceedingly simple concept, but it is not without its barriers. One barrier could be when a staff person is having a bad day (which we all have) and doesn't feel like being nice. Their car had a flat tire, they were kept up all night with child suffering from an ear infection, or they left their lunch sitting on the kitchen counter. Or maybe the visitor is in some kind of mood—parking was difficult to find and, once found, it was $20 per hour and it had started to rain.

Recognizing that there are extemporaneous circumstances that can lead to a negative baseline, very rarely will you find that your people don't know how to be nice. They usually know how because it's how they like others to treat them.

Make It Magical

"Magic" is not a word typically associated with museums, but it should be.

A good museum visit is nothing short of spectacular, enchanting even. In the definitive text for Walt Disney World's customer service approach, *Be Our Guest: Perfecting the Art of Customer Service*[9] there is a constant quest for magic. The magic of service, the magic of cast, the magic of setting, the magic of process, and the magic of integration. In pursuit of this magic, they take something that may not be explicitly magical, like a process for example, and find components within it that are.

In this sense, magic is something that happens without the customer even knowing it. Like a magic trick—it is trickery or an illusion that is carried out, purportedly, by magical means.

That may be a strange concept, because museums are seemingly not in show business. They are nonprofits, they are cultural institutions, they are community gathering places, they are educational and academic, and, yes, they are all of those things, but these elements are actually staging the experience to be had by visitors. Visitor experience staff are the stagers.

The infusion of practical magic is summed up by saying that every aspect of a visit comes together in a seamless, effortless performance. This includes all the elements of operation that add up to onstage magic. Both *Experience Economy* and *Be Our Guest* push the theater metaphor, and with good reason. We are all in the business of Broadway. No one wants to know the arduous effort it takes to make something come together, one only wants to have a nice time while experiencing the end product.

Think of seeing a movie in a movie theater. You weren't thinking about the hundreds of thousands of dollars, long cast hours, and complicated logistics behind the making of the film. You cried at the end when the heroine drank the poison because she thought she had lost her one true love, and she didn't want to live without him. That's the magic.

Leave Egos at the Door

Even with the utmost care and devotion to methods of servicing your visitor, something will go wrong, and when it does, don't be afraid to apologize.

> We will use the scar tissue from this painful mistake to help make better decisions going forward, ones that match our mission.
>
> —Jeff Bezos, Founder of Amazon[10]

For twenty years, Amazon has been a successful e-commerce company and has grown to be the largest in the world. Providing their customers with great customer service has been a pillar of their success. The company, however, originated as an online book retailer and, in 2009, when they remotely deleted copies of the books *1984* and *Animal Farm* from users' Kindles, Amazon customers experienced a side of Amazon that felt Big Brother in nature. Amazon's marketing department issued a dry and otherwise uncompelling apology, but a heartfelt apology from founder Jeff Bezos is what turned the situation around:

This is an apology for the way we previously handled illegally sold copies of *1984* and other novels on Kindle. Our "Solution" to the problem was stupid, thoughtless, and painfully out of line with our principles. It is wholly self-inflicted and we deserve the criticism we have received. We will use the scar tissue from this painful mistake to help make better decisions going forward, ones that match our mission.

With deep apology to our customers,
Jeff Bezos
Founder and CEO
Amazon.com

The outcome here is that he gave recognition to the error and promised customers that the company would learn from the mistake and not repeat it. But perhaps even more compelling than what he said was the warmth and sincerity with which he said it.

Apologizing is hard on the ego—there is vulnerability in admitting that you made a mistake. However, a solid, heartfelt apology is true representation that your organization cares about the needs of the customer. And as such, it will mean more to your visitor than most other solutions.

Service Recovery

The way your organization solves a problem can make or break the relationship that museum visitors have with the institution. This either negates or supports long-term financial sustainability by either turning them off for good or converting them into loyal guests. It's easy for frontline museum personnel and their management to believe that they are protecting the museum's bottom line by not giving things away or by putting money toward service recovery initiatives, but return on investment can be more impactful than putting money into marketing. To recover from service mishaps, workers on the front line must identify and solve customers' problems, but taking action requires decision-making and rule breaking—two things most museum employees have been conditioned against.

To believe that service recovery won't be necessary if services are executed according to their standards is to have a false sense of security. Something will go wrong, and it may be something completely out of your museum's control—bad weather, hectic traffic, lack of parking, and so on—but there is always an opportunity to make it right by providing an exclusive experience to make visitors feel heard and their frustrations validated.

Take, for example, how Club Med-Cancun treated a group of vacationers who experienced great airline setbacks upon embarking from New York on a vacation to Mexico. Their flight took off late, made several unplanned stops, and then needed to circle the airport for thirty minutes before landing. Their plane ended up being en route for so long that it ran out of food and drinks. When it finally arrived at 2 a.m., oxygen masks and luggage dropped from overhead because the landing was so bumpy. Upon exiting the plane, the travelers were understandably upset, tired, and hungry—a lawyer on board was even collecting names and addresses for a class-action lawsuit.

But the general manager of the resort the travelers were staying at while in Cancun, Silvio de Bortoli, took swift action to offset their rocky start. He appointed several staff to the airport, where they laid out food and drinks for the hungry passengers and set up a stereo system to play festive music. As the guests disembarked, they received concierge service, a sympathetic ear, and a luxurious, chauffeured ride to the resort. At Club Med, they were met with an extravagant banquet, complete with a mariachi band and champagne. The staff had even encouraged other guests to wait up to greet the newcomers, and the partying continued until sunrise. The guests were able to begin their trip on a fun note instead of a sour one. They may even have had a better experience than if their flight had gone as planned.

Although it may not be as measurable as analyzing demographic trends and ratings points, Club Med ultimately won the battle for market share that night.

It's easy to chalk upset visitors' anger up to them being "cranky," but resist that type of thinking, because no museum can afford to lose business. So, although the things that may ignite your guests' tempers sometimes seem trivial, most industry experts agree it costs much more to replace customers than it does to retain them. Museums that act like they don't care about their visitors will soon have none left, whereas those that go out of their way to exceed visitors' expectations, will soon have many more.

When service recovery goes wrong, the effects can be devastating. Consider, for instance, the case of John Barrier, a thirty-year customer of a bank in Spokane, Washington, who parked his car in a lot owned by the bank while he did business across the street. An attendant told him he could get the parking validated if he did business at the bank, even though it was not his usual branch. Barrier went into the bank and cashed a check but was eventually refused the validation because he had not made a deposit. He explained to the bank's receptionist that he was a long-time customer and had millions of dollars in the bank's accounts, but she still refused. He then explained the situation to the branch manager, but his request was denied.

The customer paid for the parking but was so angered that he drove to his home branch and explained the incident to his usual banker. Mr. Barrier requested a phone call from the executive level by the end of the day and said that if he didn't receive one, he would close all of his accounts. The call never came, and when he made his first withdrawal of $1 million, the story made national news as a model of an extreme customer service fail.

It would have cost the bank a few dollars to cover the cost of Mr. Barrier's parking, but not doing so cost them millions.

This story highlights the position of frontline employees in the making or breaking of an establishment's success. Had the bank's receptionist listened closely to the complaint, anticipated the need for recovery, acted fast, and felt empowered to close the customer feedback loop, the outcome would have been much different.

Frontline museum employees have the unique ability to head these issues off before they become too big to recover. They can look for trouble in the making by tuning in to comments made by visitors. For example, when an employee of a Marriott Hotel, which caters to business people, overheard a guest worried about the lack of privacy in the concierge lounge when he needed to hold an impromptu meeting, the hotel worker called the front desk and arranged for a vacant suite so that the meeting could be held in confidence.

Anticipating a visitor's needs before an issue is even presented, however, goes the absolute farthest. Take, for instance, this example given in a *Harvard Business Review* article on service recovery:[11]

A while back, there was a very bad fire in my house. The next day I was raking through my possessions, my family sitting on the front stoop, when a Domino's Pizza truck pulled up. The driver got out and approached us with two pizzas. I told him I didn't order any pizza and explained that our house had just burned. "I know," he replied. "I saw you when I drove by half an hour ago. I figured you must be really hungry, so my store manager and I decided to make a couple of pizzas for you. We put everything on them. If that's not how you like them, I'll take them back and get them made the way you like—on the house."

This person went on to say they would never buy pizza from any other company.

Research suggests that customers who have bad experiences tell approximately eleven people about it; those with good experiences tell just six, further illustrating the need to make the first experience a good one, and if it isn't a good one, the need to apologize and make it right. The only way to do this is to train your frontline staff to anticipate needs and empower them to do whatever they need to do to take fast action to right the wrong.

The Value of Strong Leadership

You may already have a team full of committed associates, or you may be starting from scratch. Your museum may not have a budget to employ dedicated visitor services associates, or you may have a hybrid security/experience role that fulfills servicing your guests. They may be talented, smart individuals—but are they bored? Do they need reinvigoration and excitement? Do they feel valued and essential? Are they working toward a goal?

At the Chrysler Museum of Art in Norfolk, Virginia, the registrar, webmaster, and executive assistant all consider themselves as "leaders" within the museum's staff infrastructure, according to an interview published in *Magnetic: The Art and Science of Engagement*.[12] In the museum world, academic credentials have traditionally dictated who is a leader and who isn't, but in the experiencentric, people-focused culture of the Chrysler, non-curatorial personnel are empowered to participate in their service-oriented approach to management. This results in their "leaders" feeling supported and empowered by the museum's director and board.

The team will be as good as its leader(s). It's a fundamental team-building concept to lead by example. The *New Gold Standard* outlines leadership principles to ensure a better guest experience. Many texts take this approach, mostly because in order to have a strong team, their foundation must be strong. The *New Gold Standard* highlights that good customer service starts from the top because people act in accordance with how they see those around them acting.

And it's not only in how the leadership treats museum guests, it's how they treat each other. It's how they treat the people that work for them, and how they treat the people that don't work for them—the interns and the docents, the marketing assistant, and the contract IT vendor who troubleshoots software issues during his weekly visit. All entities need to feel respected and essential in order for the museum to succeed.

Each Member of the Team is Essential

Oftentimes, more important than money is the ability for frontline staff within a museum to be able to work doing something that ignites their passion. In a study published by the *US News & World Report*,[13] the reason people work for museums and other nonprofits is because they derive an enormous amount of personal fulfillment from their work. They believe they are making a positive change in this world through their efforts. Some may think that selling tickets to a museum and providing visitors with directions and instructions on how to have the best visit are some of the most impactful things that can be done at a museum. Allowing your frontline staff to carry out the museum's "vision" in ways that are meaningful and/or pursuant to furthering their careers is critical.

You don't want anyone to feel like a "ticket-taker"; he or she is a curator of experience.

You don't want anyone to feel like a "security guard"; he or she is responsible for the safety and security, as well as the feeling of welcome, of visitors.

Giving frontline personnel projects, perhaps even ones outside of the visitor services realm, can benefit all parties involved. The frontline staff person becomes that much more invested and learns something new about the museum, and the museum has a department full of personnel they might not have tapped into to get those aspirational, on-the-horizon projects finished. A win-win.

One of the best parts of this process is that it gives the leadership an opportunity to recognize the frontline person for a job well done once the project is completed. Opportunities like this are few and far between, recognizing that comments on daily operational needs and tasks often reach the top only when they are negative, but it's far rarer, and arguably more important toward a museum's growth, for positive comments to get to the executive level.

Why is that recognition so important in the growth and success of a museum? Well, in a *Forbes* article from 2017, titled "3 Reasons Why Employee Recognition Will Always Matter,"[14] the germane benefits are discussed and are as follows.

1. When an employee is recognized, it creates happy feelings. Frontline museum staff can easily feel like no one notices the efforts they are putting forth, but when their manager shows them that their efforts are seen and appreciated—and takes the time to publicly applaud the measurable impact their efforts are having on the museum—those employees feel good about what they do and have lasting feelings of worth.

Since happy employees are, on average, 12 percent more productive than their less-happy counterparts, it can be deduced that it's to everyone's advantage when efforts are recognized.

2. Appreciative leaders make for appreciated leaders. Everyone knows that trust in the workplace is crucial, but to underline the point: trusting one another is one of the most valuable commodities a team can have.

Taking a leap of faith and building a strong foundation of trust are two strategies that can build trust at your museum, but even just the act of thanking your employees fosters an atmosphere of trust. When employees know their efforts contribute to a cause and are noticed by people higher up on the staff organizational chart, they feel a deeper connection to the institution and its mission.

Data from a study noted in the *Forbes* article indicated that nearly 90 percent of employees who received recognition or thanks from their boss in the past month showed higher levels of trust in that supervisor. Among employees who received no recognition, only 48 percent indicated that they trusted their higher-ups.

3. When employees feel recognized, they stick around.   This point considers the costs of training a brand-new employee to the point where he or she can work as assuredly as a long-tenured museum employee.

According to some estimates indicated in the article, welcoming a new hire onto the team could cost as much as $3,500 for recruitment and as much as $1,200 and thirty-two hours per year in ongoing training. All told, a new hire might cost $4,129 and as many as 42 days in lost or compromised productivity. Consider this low-cost and easy way to save your museum money and the headache of having to turn over staff, simply by giving attribution for ideas and contributions and by offering thanks.

When asked why they decided to switch to a different career, the vast majority of employees represented in a recent US Bureau of Labor and Statistics report indicated that they felt either a lack of respect or a lack of autonomy. With a little bit of recognition, you can reverse these trends and keep your talent around for much longer.

Many managers don't make recognition a priority because they don't understand its role in a thriving museum, but buy-in, empowerment, and recognition are critical, and it will be more prevalent when the experience staff feels like they have a direct influence on the outcome. The case can be made that no other staff personnel within a museum have the ability to directly affect the outcome of a visit.

The Significance in Diversity

Diversity amongst your team is critical to its success. Your visitors want to see themselves reflected in your staff and in your content—it is fundamental to the makeup of your frontline staff, so much so that there is also an entire chapter later on in this book (see chapter 3).

In a study found in *Forbes* magazine that discusses why workplace diversity is so important,[15] it's highlighted that a diverse staff offers your organization a wider pool of talent and provides insight into the needs and motivations of your visitors. Potentially, as McKinsey & Company and a host of other highly credible research companies have shown, it can make your organization more effective, more successful, and more profitable.

Despite a sincere desire on the part of organizations to implement effective diversity strategies, few have come up with actionable strategies. A deeper dive into why provides the following insights: there is a disparity between how organizations design diversity policies and how they implement them, meaning what looks good on paper doesn't work in practice; and there is a failure to align diversity practices with organizational goals. So, no matter how much goodwill there is toward the concept of diversity, keeping up with operations, maintaining customer satisfaction, and selling and delivering the product or service will take precedence.

The *Forbes* study identified four clear steps toward making workplace diversity a reality:

1. *Identify measurable objectives.* Often, diversity initiatives miss their intended mark. Museums aim to realize the performance potential of diverse teams but then implement diversity policies primarily designed to impact the representation of certain social groups. Understand what the goal is and what will signify that you have reached it.
2. *Make it your own.* Every museum is unique, so their diversity initiatives need to be, too. Borrowing one from somewhere else won't work, because each program should speak to the specific culture and context of its host organization.
3. *Good design is important, but good implementation is vital.* In the military, there is a saying: "No plan survives contact with the enemy." And without comprehensive training and concerted effort, few diversity initiatives will survive contact with your museum frontline staff. Even the best designed program won't be effective if the individuals charged with implementation—your museum's guest experience personnel—don't possess the ability, tools, or desire.
4. *Figure out the "Why?"* Successful initiatives answer the basic question, Why should I do this? Individuals within the museum need to understand the essentiality for a program to take hold.

Actualized workplace diversity is so significant that the challenges inherent to it must be resolved.

The Need for Balance

An effective team is well-balanced. Someone needs to be taking care of administration, someone needs to attend to operations, someone needs to be tailoring visitor approach, and someone needs to be careful about sales. Guest experience is an area that is comprised of many sub-departments, which, for many, is its allure.

Natural ability will arise, and the key is to maximize your talent by letting them do what they do best. And it may not always be in the guest experience department. Hiring and retaining experienced staff becomes an organic "recruitment" process for the entire museum as different strengths rise to the surface. And this is a good thing! Hiring someone, moving them through your training program to be wildly successful in a visitor experience capacity, to have them subsequently move into a curatorial or education position may feel like a failure, but it means you have hired and retained talent for your organization. Be proud of yourself for having a keen eye and being the person who supplies your institution with an endless stream of talent. And amongst that talent, you will find some who want to be in visitor experience because they recognize the impact they can have on the success of the institution. Those are your people.

Remain Supportive Through It All

Customer service is hard. The easiest way to get your staff to be nice is to remove controllable barriers to their ability to put their best foot forward. A supportive relationship between manager and employee, a flexible (or at least, fair) work policy when available, open communication flow, and other elements allow the employee to not feel logistically tapped and allow them to focus all their efforts into being the best employee they can be while at work.

Efforts at building up your staff will result in an increase in commitment, and enhancing customer service starts with your team. Along with the following five techniques, communication and teaching leadership are integral ways to enhance the customer experience.[16]

1. Coach, don't tell. Remember a time you were told to do something. Now remember a time where someone asked you to look at a situation, think about it critically, and asked what you thought should be done about it.

Asking your frontline staff about what they are seeing or noticing about the guest experience or the volume of business, or asking them if they could have done things differently, helps them problem-solve as it relates to your museum's set mission, vision, and values. It's much easier to tell your team what to do—but it's more effective to involve them in the process and let them know you value their thoughts.

2. Not everything is said out loud.   When you not only teach job skills but also communication and life skills, you empower your staff to treat your customers better. By paying close attention to body language and tone of voice, you can learn more about how a guest feels about their experience. If something is wrong, your customers or guests may not say so, but if their smiles have subsided or their voices have changed, that might suggest otherwise. Teaching nonverbal communication skills improves customer service because it opens an opportunity to focus on the guest's needs.

3. Openly reward positive behavior.   People learn from demonstrated successful behavior. It's important to train guest experience staff in traditional ways, but another way the team learns is by watching the behaviors of others. Encourage supervisors to openly reward and recognize a job well done in front of other team members and executive staff. It helps create a healthy sense of competition and the motivation to perform better and earn the same recognition.

4. Change is hard, but it's good.   When new team members are hired, it's normal for worry to take hold, especially if things are currently going well. We know that an experiencentric team is a balanced team, and adding a new personality with new skill sets can be a daunting moment for a team that is comfortable with their current equilibrium. Introduce a new team member on their first day to everyone within the organization to help both sides feel comfortable. Have them work with the same trainer each day of their training, if possible. A standardized training process will put both the current staff and the person being trained at ease because then it becomes a familiar and time-proven process in a time of uncertainty.

5. Discourage drama.   Teach your visitor experience staff to be aware of how we create drama within ourselves and with others. Drama is caused by gossip, anxiety, and worry about the future, the past, and the things over which we have no control. Encourage your team members to focus on the present. By diminishing the percentage of time your visitor experience staff is engaged in "drama," they will have more time to spend connecting with guests.

Imagine a stranger arrives at your front door, bearing a map and asking for directions to the nearest grocery store. How might you treat that person? Now envision your oldest friend knocks on your door, one you haven't seen in a few years and that lives in a faraway city—how would you treat that person? Which person is going to feel more like they belong in your home? More warmly accepted? Who is going to want to pull up a chair and stay awhile? With the vision and team aligned, visitors find the experience they are after and feel like they are that friend.

The Visitor Experience Group

Did you know there is a professional development group geared specifically toward visitor experience professionals in museums and other cultural attractions?

They are the Visitor Experience Group, or VEX for short. They even have an annual conference! The 2020 conference was virtual, due to COVID-19, and included timely visitor experience topics including the following:

- "Strength in Differences: The Well-Rounded Team" (presented by the Albright-Knox Art Gallery)
- "Becoming Learner Centered" (presented by the Museum of Contemporary Art Cleveland)
- "So What? Using Themes to Improve All Aspects of Visitor Experience" (presented by the Royal Botanic Gardens)
- "Setting the Example from the Top Down: Employee Engagement for Part-Time Teams" (presented by Longwood Gardens)
- "Want to Make Meaningful Connections with Visitors? Start Training Staff for Empathy" (presented by President Lincoln's Cottage)
- "From Anecdote to Action: Turning Online Reviews into Actionable Data Using Sentiment Analysis" (presented by the Lowell Observatory)

VEX is comprised of a group of volunteers (more than two thousand followers and growing) who are dedicated to improving the field through the programs we offer.

The VEX Mission

To provide leadership, support, and professional development and encourage collaboration in the areas of Guest Services, Audience Engagement, and Operations.

The VEX Vision

All cultural institutions recognize and promote the importance of the visitor experience.

VEX Values

SERVICE + ENGAGEMENT = EXPERIENCE
- Proactive, quality service combined with meaningful, attentive engagement, leads to exceptional experiences for visitors and staff.

INTEGRITY
- We believe hiring practices should be transparent and all job postings should include accurate salary ranges.
- Museum leadership needs to include front of house representation.

INCLUSION
- In our work we strive to bring attention to inequities in the cultural sector and encourage institutions to actively pursue a more inclusive, accessible, diverse, and equitable workforce.
- We believe in a people-first approach—institutions are nothing without the people whose work propels and upholds the mission.
- We strive to provide a platform to amplify diverse voices in our field.
- We seek to promote diversity, equity, inclusion, and accessibility in the policies, practices, operations, and organizational culture of the cultural organizations that VEX serves.
- We advocate to increase the diversity of representation at every level of the organization we serve, and for the strategic recruitment of persons of color and amplify their voices in decision making.
- We strive for racial justice and to actively promote anti-racist methodologies.

INGENUITY
- Quality work happens when creativity is encouraged and supported with appropriate resources.
- We believe in the power of change and leading that change as innovators in the field and through the promotion of best practices.
- We recognize that the best ideas come from diversity in people and experiences.

TEAMWORK
- We believe in collaboration between individuals, institutions, and within the community at large.
- We believe that a fun, safe, and engaging work environment leads to quality experiences for guests and staff.

We believe that guest services are one of the fundamental priorities of any cultural organization.

To find out more visit: visitorexperience.group or access session videos from past annual conferences on their YouTube channel.

Notes

1. Prentice, Richard. "Managing Implosion: The Facilitation of Insight through the Provision of Context." *Museum Management and Curatorship* 25, no. 2 (1996): 169–85.

2. Pine II, B. Joseph, and James H. Gilmore. *The Experience Economy: Work Is Theater and Every Business Is a Stage* Boston, MA: Harvard Business Review Press, 2011.

3. Mody, Makarand, and Monica Gomez. "Airbnb and the Hotel Industry: The Past, Present, and Future of Sales, Marketing, Branding, and Revenue Management." *Boston Hospitality Review* (Fall 2018). https://www.bu.edu/bhr/2018/10/31/airbnb-and-the-hotel-industry-the-past-present-and-future-of-sales-marketing-branding-and-revenue-management/.

4. Pine, B. Joseph, and James H. Gilmore. "Welcome to the Experience Economy." *Harvard Business Review* (July-August 1998). Accessed August 1, 2014. https://hbr.org/1998/07/welcome-to-the-experience-economy. n.p.

5. Michelli, Joseph A. *The New Gold Standard: 5 Leadership Principles for Creating a Legendary Customer Experience Courtesy of the Ritz-Carlton Hotel Company.* New York: McGraw-Hill, 2008.

6. Wilder, Kelly, Joel Collier, and Donald Barnes. "Tailoring to Customers' Needs: Understanding How to Promote an Adaptive Service Experience with Frontline Employees." *Journal of Service Research* 17 (2014): 446–59.

7. Paiva, Tiago. "Will AI Replace Humans in the Customer Service Industry?" *Forbes*, August 10, 2017. https://www.forbes.com/sites/valleyvoices/2017/08/10/will-ai-replace-humans-in-the-customer-service-industry/?sh=6636592d93c4.

8. Paiva. "Will AI Replace Humans in the Customer Service Industry?"

9. Kinni, Theodore B. *Be Our Guest: Perfecting the Art of Customer Service.* New York: Disney Editions, 2011.

10. Baldacci, Kevin. "7 Customer Service Lessons from Amazon CEO Jeff Bezos." *Salesforce* (blog), June 10, 2013 Accessed March 9, 2020. https://www.salesforce.com/blog/2013/06/jeff-bezos-lessons.html.

11. Hart, Christopher W., James L. Heskitt, and W. Earl Sasser. "The Profitable Art of Service Recovery." *Harvard Business Review* (July-August, 1990).https://hbr.org/1990/07/the-profitable-art-of-service-recovery.

12. Bergeron, Anne, and Beth Tuttle. "Case Study: The Chrysler Museum of Art." Chapter in *Magnetic: The Art and Science of Engagement*, by Anne Bergeron and Beth Tuttle. Arlington, VA: American Alliance of Museums Press, 2013, 99.

13. Green, Alison. "Thinking About a Nonprofit Job? Here's What You Should Know." *US News & World Report*, March 26, 2014. Accessed March 9, 2020. https://money.usnews.com/money/blogs/outside-voices-careers/2014/03/26/thinking-about-a-nonprofit-job-heres-what-you-should-know.

14. Craig, William. "3 Reasons Why Employee Recognition Will Always Matter." *Forbes*, July 17, 2017. https://www.forbes.com/sites/williamcraig/2017/07/17/3-reasons-why-employee-recognition-will-always-matter/?sh=18149d6a63c9.

15. Shemla, Meir. "Why Workplace Diversity Is So Important, and Why It's So Hard to Achieve." *Forbes*, August 22, 2018. https://www.forbes.com/sites/rsmdiscovery/2018/08/22/why-workplace-diversity-is-so-important-and-why-its-so-hard-to-achieve/#4810cbe33096.

16. Sarillo, Nicholas. "5 Ways to Support Your Customers by Supporting Your Staff." *Trends and Insights—Customer Service*, American Express (website), February 15, 2013. Accessed March 9, 2020. https://www.americanexpress.com/en-us/business/trends-and-insights/articles/back-to-school-support-your-customers-by-supporting-your-staff/.

2

A Whole-Museum Commitment to Service

THERE ARE MANY DEPARTMENTS within a museum, and how well they work with and support the visitor experience team is vital in honoring a culture of service. A true service culture doesn't only have to do with museum guests; it extends to all museum staff and their commitment to serve. In this chapter, we will examine the entire organization being committed to service and why this will set the stage for positive interaction with your museum visitors.

A culture of service is an idea that the culture within your organization prioritizes service to one another. It's a collective thought process about being obsessed with customer service, so much so that it even comes across in the way you treat the people with whom you work.

Attention to the service environment makes sense in any museum.

In her article from *Forum* magazine, "Because It Just Makes Sense: Serving the Museum Visitor,"[1] Kathryn Hill explores why establishing service to visitors as an institution-wide priority is necessary. The service environment encompasses a wide array of elements outside of exhibitions and education programs that impact the quality of a museum visit. Signage, food and beverage, building and exhibit maintenance, and employee friendliness are all examples of fundamental elements of a museum visit, and if those fundamentals have not been satisfied, visitors will not be likely to embark on intellectual pursuits. Hill likens it to Maslow's hierarchy of needs, but it's also common sense. Visitors won't learn if they can't find the bathroom. This moves the urgency of a positive visitor experience from the background to the center—the mission demands it.

The frontline staff represents an organization to the public, and our missions are to educate our public. So then, how we treat our frontline staff will be reflected in how they treat our visitors. Since our missions are to educate, we cannot fulfill our missions if we are not serving visitors. We cannot thrive if we don't serve visitors well because the sustainability of our museums depends on it. So, we must act in the best interest of our employees to be in the full best interest of our visitors; but, how do we do that?

This chapter will discuss how to grow a service-oriented culture and will investigate its importance. It will talk about empathetic communication and the leadership's role in fostering a service culture, and then will conclude with why it's the entire museum's responsibility.

How to Grow a Culture of Service

In a 2018 *Forbes* magazine article on how to promote a positive workplace culture,[2] Alan Kohll highlights that as long as employers take the time to genuinely invest in the happiness and well-being of their workforce, a positive service culture can be grown in any museum, with any budget.

Here are some steps you can take to grow a positive service-oriented culture within your organization:

1. *Provide purpose.* Especially in the nonprofit museum space, meaning and purpose can be more important than money. The majority of nonprofit employees are there because they prioritize meaning and purpose in their work. And a museum can't build a culture without meaning. Make sure your visitor experience staff knows your mission and purpose, and connect them to specific examples of how their roles positively impact the museum and its visitors.
2. *Put positivity first.* Encourage positivity in the workplace. Leaders should express gratitude, smile frequently, and remain optimistic during difficult situations. Fellow museum staff, as well as any visitors faced with a challenge, are more likely to respond positively to a situation when they are seeing others around them responding positively.
3. *Grow your current culture.* To keep costs to a minimum, museums should work on enhancing their current culture. Ask employees what they do and don't like about their current culture and work environment. Leaders can use these suggestions to help reformulate a culture that reflects their needs. This is a key customer service element—listening to feedback and letting the customers (or in this case, employees) know they are being heard—so be a good listener. Being a good listener

is one of the easiest ways to tap into trust. Make sure everyone in the museum feels their voices are heard and valued, and that will lead to mutual respect and beneficial outcomes.

4. *Be goal-oriented.* No organization can host a strong culture without clear goals in place. Creating service-oriented goals and objectives will foster a museum-wide service culture that brings people together and gives everyone something specific to work toward.

5. *Encourage Service Stars.* "Service Stars" are employees who embody the values and missions of a company. They are excited to promote the museums' commitment to service and encourage others to do the same. Identify these employees and encourage them because positivity leads to more positivity. It's contagious.

6. *Cultivate community.* Workplace relationships are key to a positive corporate culture. Staff need to interact to provide service to one another. Anyone will be more apt to serve someone to whom they feel personally connected, and providing opportunities to connect is crucial. Consider weekly team brown-bag lunches, a 3 p.m. afternoon group walk-around, or even a book club to get things started.

7. *Emphasize employee wellness.* Healthy employees are needed to have a healthy organization. When employees feel their best physically, mentally, and emotionally, they will be better suited to contribute to a positive corporate culture. It feels good to know that your employer cares about you as a person rather than only about your output.

By building your brand of service culture, you will strengthen the ties that bind and ensure a positive culture that enhances the talent within your museum.

Visitor Services as a Liaison

The connectors. The facilitators. The enhancers. The stagers. Frontline museum staff can take exhibit and program development to the next level by providing observations of visitor behavior. Front-of-house team members can be your eyes and ears! Invite your visitors to stop by the desk or email the visitor services management with any suggestions. Everyone wins with this strategy, because visitors feel heard, valued, and that they are helping to advise the success of the organization, while management is able to take action on their perceptions.

When contemplating content creation, it would be most helpful to know what your visitors want, and the people interacting with museum visitors have this insight. They can peek into visitors' thoughts through observation and conversation—finding out what they liked and, perhaps more importantly, what they didn't like. Members of a curatorial team would be wise to enlist this visitor experience acumen.

Kyle Cantarera, guest experience manager at Mt. Cuba Center in Hockessin, Delaware, and hospitality chairperson of VEX (the Visitor Experience Group), describes an out-of-the-box initiative through which guest experience staff are gauging interaction with the botanical garden.

> Every half hour when the gardens are open for general admission, our public safety team will travel through the guest parking lot and document the location of cars parked in the lot. They record this data on a tablet that feeds to a spreadsheet. From there, we can ascertain guest length of stay as well as parking lot turnover. Because the data is parking space specific, we are also able to use it to determine which spaces in the lot are the most popular.

When asked about the origins of the initiative, Cantarera says,

> Mt. Cuba Center's visitation has continued to grow over the last seven years, but it took its first significant jump in 2017, and our parking capacity quickly became a point of discussion. We had room in the gardens to handle more visitation, but the pinch point was parking. We needed to know when our parking lot was the busiest to help inform our staffing and programming schedules. Our leadership team also requested the data to help them plan for the construction of a new parking lot—when and how big? The guest experience department developed the procedures and maintains the data as both public safety and visitor data collection/analysis are housed in our department.

Regarding whether the program has thus far produced a viable solution to the original problem, Cantarera replies,

> Thus far, with two years of data (2018 and 2019), the collection of it has already paid dividends with the potential to provide even more. The leadership team used the information to decide on the size of the new parking lot which is to be constructed next year, and our programming and interpretation team has been able to use the length of stay comparisons as a metric to measure how successful their efforts are at engaging guests, since a longer visit often means a more engaged visit.

Frontline staff can also play the extremely important role of heading off negative comments before they can be shared with a broader, more reputation-damaging audience. They are who will most directly affect your Trip Advisor, Google, Facebook, and Yelp reviews, which play an ever more popular role in potential visitors' decisions about where to spend their precious free time.

Traditionally, within a museum setting, academic credentials are of primary importance. Someone needs to curate, to design the exhibits, and to be the research fellow. However, someone needs to interact with the people, or else all of those other activities don't matter, and that's where guest experience comes in. There is beauty in frontline visitor experience staff; anyone who has experienced service well-done is a candidate to produce good service.

The Importance of Empathetic Interdepartmental Communication

Even if they get along well, curatorial, collections, marketing, and education departments often have a hard time understanding one another. When focused on a particular perspective within an organization, each department thinks and operates in its own set way. Many times, these fixed attitudes and procedures run counter to how those in other departments function. Various departments work within each other's landscapes, and this creates friction and puts a strain on communication.

Cynthia Helmstetter, visitor engagement manager at the Museum of the American Revolution in Philadelphia, Pennsylvania and events chairperson of VEX, speaks of an initiative they practice to work against this kind of siloed operation. She explains,

> Our VEAs [visitor engagement associates] interview staff across all departments. The program was developed when the museum opened in 2017 and was intended to break down barriers between the frontline and back of house staff. From previous jobs I have held, I understood the need to foster respect and understanding between these groups. When everyone knows the importance of each other's responsibilities, respectful relationships are created. There is a sense of, "we are all in this together" amongst the whole staff. I make Outlook calendar invitations between the back of house staff members and the VEAs during museum hours, and the meetings are scheduled for thirty minutes.

Helmstetter notes, interview questions include:

- Why did you decide to become a curator?
- How much schooling did you complete?
- What are your interests outside of the museum?
- What questions do you find guests ask all the time?

She continues,

> We have found the program cultivates respect between back of house and frontline staff. In addition, the VEAs learn about skills that are used by staff in many

departments including: membership, development, operations, and education. The VEAs use the findings from the interviews to aid in their decisions about whether or not to go to graduate school, museum career path, and sometimes to enrich their curiosity about how everyone contributes to the success of the museum.

Helmstetter says the need that was previously identified was answered, because "yearly staff surveys show that frontline staff now feel more valued. Also, the administrative staff gets to know the VEAs by name, making the whole organization more cohesive."

The importance of interdepartmental communication is well-known, but Danny Wong, the co-founder of Blank Label, an award-winning luxury menswear company, drills down on specific problems that can occur and how empathetic communication can solve such issues, in an article that appeared in the *HuffPost* in 2015.[3] Reframed for museums, these same principles apply:

Different departments need your context, so that they understand the ideas. When half of a meeting's attendees don't understand what is happening, productivity suffers. To keep everyone functioning their best, it is important to provide context that can put everyone on the same page.

During meetings or interactions, illustrate for your colleagues what the organization-wide desired outcome would be in a way that everyone can appreciate. This allows everyone to be able to actively engage in the conversation because they understand it.

Put yourself in their shoes. An important part of fostering stronger interdepartmental communications is mutual understanding. Ask yourself questions about the pressure that others might feel or how it affects their workload.

Practicing empathy shows support and that you care about one another, which means the team will collectively be better equipped to seek long-term results.

Recognize teachable moments. Openly admit when you don't understand a train of thought; it's a healthy part of the learning process. No one should fault you for requesting clarity about a conversation, email thread, or project; rather, it means you are listening to them and are invested in what they are saying. Most will take that as a compliment.

By not minimizing your co-workers' confusion and instead appreciating that they are attempting to understand, you will strengthen the collective ability to respond effectively to change and remain resilient through challenges.

Don't take it personally. Constructive dialogue is a component of the critical thought process. Unsupportive behavior and invalidating responses drive resentment—better problem-solving will result from allowing people to disagree and express emotions.

Encouraging the team to be receptive to interdepartmental communication will also amount to a better discussion. Prioritizing organizational goals will be key to everyone keeping an open mind and not feeling offended when someone disagrees with your idea.

Encourage Social Interaction. Cliques happen everywhere and it's easy to enter a meeting and sit next to your department mates—it's common to see co-workers hanging out with their peers from the same departments. To advocate for a more collaborative environment, create situations that encourage intermingling. You can do this by assigning seats or mixing them up, encouraging lunch meetings, starting a mentoring program, or allowing off-site meetings.

Keep everyone on the same page. If departments use jargon specific to their work, it will be hard to have effective cross-departmental communication. Use verbiage that everyone recognizes to ensure that people fully understand the issues at hand and can honestly give their feedback in a meaningful way.

At Grounds for Sculpture, in Hamilton New Jersey, they use Microsoft Teams to communicate between frontline managers and administrative staff. Manager of guest services and VEX events committee member Mark Baird explains,

> We have always had a subscription to Microsoft products, but we mostly just used Word, Excel, and PowerPoint. Teams was a part of the Microsoft Suite, but nobody used it. During the COVID-19 quarantine, our director of guest services started using it with our finance and human resources departments, and once we learned how useful it was, we integrated it as a communication system.

Baird said he makes videos through PowerPoint, to train on how to use Microsoft Teams. He explained:

> There is a part of Teams which allows someone to make a video with a voiceover while you record your screen. I enlarged my mouse to allow the user to see it clearly. It allows me to personalize them for our institution. There are a lot of training videos for the service online but some are outdated, so I found it more useful to tailor make our own.

When asked if it was a difficult learning curve for the staff, he answers,

> Any new software or platform takes time for individuals to learn how to use the software in a way that will benefit the collective organization. Teams has a chat function which is really helpful. There is also a discussion board function for specific topics.

Overall, Baird says Microsoft Teams is a great place to organize projects your team is working on:

> It can organize and store files for you and has a variety of separate apps that you can integrate with so it benefits for your organization. There are hundreds of apps to choose from. With many of our meetings becoming virtual, Teams is a great place to set up a meeting time and place and use Zoom-like program. An added bonus is that it clears up our email for only communication outside of our organization; Teams is used internally.

Respond with Empathy. To minimize misinterpretation, be aware of varying communication styles and understand how to speak the language of those you are communicating with. Some tips for clear communication interdepartmentally are as follows:

- When replying to an email, save it as a draft to review five minutes later, asking yourself if you addressed the questions asked and offered useful information.
- Evaluate if a response is better handled by phone, in person, or via email. Interpersonal contact can allow for nuances to be understood that writing cannot convey. If need be, follow up with a confirmation email summarizing what was discussed.
- Sometimes the way that you communicate—your tone of voice, inflection, and body language—can be as important as your content, and a discussion, rather than a directive, will go a long way.

The Museum Director's Role

Software giant Microsoft's CEO, Satya Nadella, joined the company in 1992. He began his tenure with the company as a twenty-five-year-old engineer and earned his MBA while working for Microsoft full time. While Microsoft may seem far different from a museum, the inherent leadership principles that have helped him rise to success are not.

Speaking at a Mobile World Congress (MWC) conference in Barcelona in February of 2019, Nadella explained how he evaluates both exemplary leadership in the candidates that he hires as well as traits he looks to nurture within himself.[4] His top three leadership qualities are as follows:

1. *A leader should provide clarity.* In times of crisis or chaos, those who can offer clarity and help ease a difficult situation are the leaders. "Leaders have this amazing, uncanny capability of bringing clarity into a situation where none exists," Nadella said. "You can't call yourself a leader by coming into a situation that is by nature uncertain or ambiguous—and create confusion," he stated in Barcelona, adding that to be a leader, you "have to create clarity where none exists." Nadella has been quoted saying that "this is the most important attribute that any kind of leader should have, yet it can often be underestimated."

   Nonprofit museums inevitably harbor a predisposition for financial issues, and it's beneficial to have leadership that can guide the museum through times of financial or external crisis with clarity and focus.

2. *A leader should generate energy.* For Microsoft's chief executive, having genuine passion and enthusiasm for what you do is of critical importance. "Leaders create energy," Nadella said, adding that if a person comes up to you and says, 'I'm great, my team is great, everybody else around me sucks,' that person is not a leader." "You have to create energy all around you," said Nadella, building upon comments he made in Chicago last year, where he explained that you have to "be at your evangelical best. You have got to have followership all around you."

   This energy will sustain the museum, even in indirect ways. The energy of the CEO role will be felt and duplicated by the visitor experience staff, who will then pass it on to the visitors.

3. *Leaders should drive success—in any condition.* Leadership is not a fair-weather friend. "The last thing is that leaders have to drive success in—what is essentially—an over-constrained problem," Nadella added. "You can't say, 'I'm waiting for the perfect weather and the full alignment of stars, and I'll show you my brilliance.' I mean, that's not leadership. . . . You have to be able to figure it out and drive success."

   Driving success in museums will look different to each institution, but no matter what it is that defines your organization's success, having a leader that supports efforts toward achieving that success is critical.

And so, these are some key aspects Microsoft takes into account when looking at job applicants. Microsoft encourages its employees to pursue their passions and embrace their own identities. The company states that it's looking for people who have a "strong desire to learn, intelligence, a passion for technology, a willingness to work hard, rock-solid skills, an entrepreneurial spirit, and a desire to be the best."

"Ultimately, it's understandable if you fail to hit top form for all three elements, all the time," Nadella concluded in his speech. "It's trying your best and learning from mistakes that matters. . . . To do these three things well and not have hubris is what I think you need in leaders. . . . You've got to start by—someone like me—acknowledging that I'm not perfect on those three all the time and [so I] push myself to learn."

Every Department is Important to the Success of the Institution

With guest experience emerging as a foundational department within the framework of a museum's organizational chart, and with more museums recognizing that balance is crucial, and all parts of a team have equal weight, the recognition of just how important the experience a museum visitor has is becoming a primary focus for financial sustainability.

At ticket sales giant Stubhub.com,[5] they have a couple of teamwork philosophies that are worth sharing because they can be closely modeled at any visitor services desk. Stubhub.com encourages high-trust teams with their three points of the pyramid model. They have designed a concept where the literal and figurative pinnacle is their "North Star" of customer outcomes and success metrics.

To execute against the North Star, they enforce three parts of the pyramid.

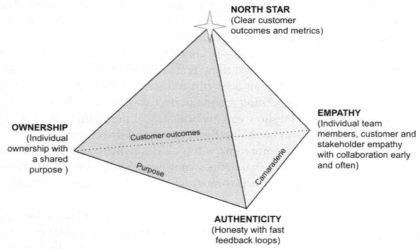

FIGURE 2.1
The "North Star" of customer service.
Source: Lau (2018).[6]

1. *Ownership.* Every person, no matter the role they play on the Stubhub .com team, needs to feel proud of the team's outcomes. The goal is for the Stubhub.com teammates to look at their "product" and feel like they were a part of the crew that successfully built the end product.

   In a museum setting, the visitor experience staff should feel a sense of ownership about the museum, and they should want to "show it off" to visitors. It can be challenging to give experience staff this kind of pride, because, historically, they have not been involved in the content creation; however, this is an opportunity to challenge the norm and make them a part of it, with great benefit.

2. *Authenticity.* Stubhub.com employees are asked to be their most genuine selves. "Witty, goofy, risky, driven, risk-averse, and stubborn—these are a few differences that can make a team stronger. We can't have all defenders or all goal-scorers on the team, just as we can't have all risk-taking or visionary people on the team," said Jennifer Lau, a senior product manager with Stubhub.com.[7] Valuing differences amongst the team members will make it stronger because each person brings a perspective to the table.

3. *Empathy.* Perhaps the most important of the three points of the pyramid is empathy. The team must have empathy for each other, for their customers, and for stakeholders. Similarly, within a museum, visitor experience staff should respect one another, respect the visitors, and respect the executive management. Respecting one another and understanding why various perspectives all have equal importance propels the team toward the goal of visitor satisfaction rather than dwelling on impact to the business.

Within the framework of a museum, it's not exclusively up to the visitor experience staff to care about the business impact of their work. At the same time, it's not the curator's sole duty to care about what visitors want to see, and it's not up to the facilities department alone to care about technical feasibility. When there are feelings of shared ownership, the team has a more unified approach overall.

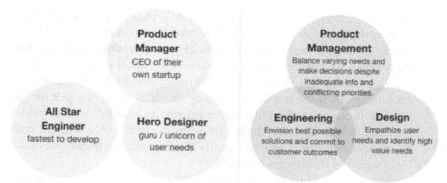

FIGURE 2.2
Shared ownership equals a more unified approach.
Above left: **a conventional view of a high-functioning team.** *Above right:* **how a truly balanced team with shared ownership looks.**
Source: Lau (2019).[8]

Supporting the Framework

This chapter hasn't dealt with the inner workings of visitor services staff, but it's important to highlight that without a supportive and cohesive organizational framework at your organization even a highly successful visitor experience department will fail. Creating a service culture, communicating with empathy, having strong and supportive leadership, and working well together as a team, are all critical elements of any experience philosophy.

Notes

1. Hill, Kathryn, "Because It Just Makes Sense: Serving the Museum Visitor," *Forum*, 1993.

2. Kohll, Alan. "How to Build a Positive Company Culture." *Forbes*, August 14, 2018. https://www.forbes.com/sites/alankohll/2018/08/14/how-to-build-a-positive-company-culture/#412016ac49b5.

3. Wong, Danny. "How to Improve Interdepartmental Collaboration." *HuffPost*, September 15, 2015. Last updated December 6, 2017. https://www.huffpost.com/entry/how-to-improve-interdepar_b_8128368.

4. Gibbs, Alexandra. "Microsoft CEO Satya Nadella on the 3 Qualities That Make a Great Leader." *Yahoo! Finance*, February 26, 2019. https://finance.yahoo.com/news/microsoft-ceo-satya-nadella-3-120555164.html.

5. Lau, Jennifer. "How We Build and Sustain High-Trust Teams." *Product & Tech* (blog), Stubhub, December 20, 2018. Accessed January 16, 2019. https://

medium.com/stubhub-product-tech-blog/how-we-build-and-sustain-high-trust
-teams-e51e5d886d20.

6. Lau. "How We Build and Sustain High-Trust Teams."
7. Lau. "How We Build and Sustain High-Trust Teams."
8. Lau. "How We Build and Sustain High-Trust Teams."

3

Experience Staff as DEAI Advocates

D IVERSITY, EQUITY, ACCESSIBILITY, AND INCLUSION (DEAI) requires top-of-mind awareness when creating a visitor experience philosophy and should be at the forefront of all visitor experience efforts. The essence of a positive experience is to exceed the standards of comfort for guests, so a lack of inclusivity or accessibility will hugely impact the way visitors feel during their visit.

As a community gathering place, a museum has a responsibility to its entire community. This topic is vast, with many layers, so this chapter will mostly look at the way DEAI and service philosophy are interrelated.

In this chapter, we will discuss:

- the need for frontline staff to effectively impart DEAI initiatives, and why this is the responsibility of visitor services;
- the breadth of being of an inclusive community gathering place;
- thinking of your visitors as individuals and centralizing DEAI into the everyday operation;
- visitor services specific initiatives;
- your visitor services staff being diverse, inclusive, and equal; and
- recommended texts and works on this subject as it pertains to the museum field.

Achieving comprehensive inclusion is an ongoing effort and one that requires pursuit with the same vigor and passion that museums have historically brought to collecting, interpreting, and educating—it's a core element of activating any museum's mission.

DEAI as Visitor Services' Responsibility

DEAI initiatives are a whole museum effort, but for those directly interfacing with your visitors it's a primary focus.

Think about a time you felt unwelcome somewhere. Why would you want to spend your precious free time or hard-earned money there? You wouldn't. So, then it's no surprise that there's absolutely no way you'd be comfortable enough in that place to interpret information, learn, and/or connect.

For these reasons (and many more), a museum that doesn't practice equality isn't accessible, isn't inclusive, and will not be able to fulfill its mission. Mission fulfillment aside, it's also unlikely that a museum will perform at its maximum capability under those conditions. According to the McKinsey Foundation, gender-diverse companies are 15 percent more likely to outperform competitors, and those that are ethnically diverse are 35 percent more likely to outperform.[1]

Program staff has a responsibility to plan programs for all, and the curatorial team must design inclusive exhibits. While the rest of your museum staff focuses their efforts on their respective departments, it is the responsibility of the visitor experience staff to communicate them. After all, serving visitors is our actual job.

The True Meaning of a Community Gathering Place

Our common humanity. The ways we are different and the ways we are the same. The full spectrum of this human possibility is found in any community. To whom does your museum belong? What takes place there? What stories are we telling?

Answering these questions requires introspection and dedicated effort. And it cannot be assumed that untrained museum professionals know how to approach this work.

In the 2018 "Facing Change: Insights from the American Alliance of Museums' Diversity, Equity, Accessibility, and Inclusion Working Group" report,[2] insights on particular elements of effective DEAI strategy were pinpointed and when interpreted through a visitor experience lens, they could prove very helpful.

Insight: Every museum professional must do personal work to face unconscious bias.

Unconscious bias includes the automatic, often unspoken beliefs about a given social group—that has the power to influence every aspect of a museum. Everyone has them because the urge to evaluate is a natural human response. Social and behavioral scientists note that the "ability to distinguish friend from foe helped early humans survive."

A study on the commitment to lessening bias in the workplace, by Boston Consulting Group,[3] found that all diverse groups studied (women, LGBTQ employees, and people of color) rated a bias-free day-to-day experience as one of the most effective interventions for improving DEAI—and frontline leaders are the people most directly positioned to control this. When frontline leaders commit, employees in underrepresented groups are far more likely to say that their day-to-day experience is free of bias and that they do not perceive obstacles in recruiting, retention, advancement, and leadership commitment.

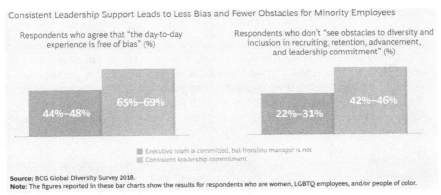

Source: BCG Global Diversity Survey 2018.
Note: The figures reported in these bar charts show the results for respondents who are women, LGBTQ employees, and/or people of color.

FIGURE 3.1
Leadership support leads to less obstacles.
Source: Garcia-Alonso, Matt Krentz, and Poulsen (2020).[4]

Since biases have the power to influence all aspects of a museum's operation, the importance of identifying them is critical for heading them off before acting on them. By actively being aware of bias, you may work toward managing it through empathy and action-oriented strategy. From a visitor experience perspective, this self-work can be addressed at each interaction. However, the expectation is to not assume that this can be accomplished without expert help and training.

What you can do: This work is best fulfilled, if possible, by an outside facilitator.

If an external facilitator is not an option, you can also take the Harvard Implicit Association Test for free, online,[5] to help identify your own unconscious biases and suggest your co-workers or visitor services team do the same. You can then host a brown-bag lunch gathering to discuss your findings and agree to share your results via a safe and respectful conversation.

Insight: Inclusion is central to the effectiveness and sustainability of museums.

The future of a museum's sustainability rests with its visitors and its communities. So, a museum's ability to be financially sustainable rests within that museum's ability to be as inclusive as possible.

Museums will need to cultivate practices that effect change. Through their physical space, exhibitions, and programs, museums inspire and educate. They also support local and national economies—to the tune of $50 billion GDP in the United States in 2016, according to recent research by AAM and Oxford Economics.[6] Despite this broad reach, museum staff and visitors require further diversification.

> Although nonwhite people make up 23 percent of the overall US population, they comprise only 9 percent of museum visitorship. African Americans hold only 4 percent of the leadership positions in US art museums; Latinx professionals hold only 3 percent of total leadership jobs in the sector. The 2017 Museum Board Leadership report, published by AAM in partnership with nonprofit leadership organization BoardSource, revealed that 46 percent of museum boards are all white.[7]

National trends demonstrate a growing diversity of data regarding ability, age, gender identity, sexual orientation, race, and ethnicity in the United States, and if museums want to continue to receive both the financial support and affection of their audiences, they will need to reflect the demographics of the communities they serve.

At the 2015 AAM Annual Meeting, Dr. Johnnetta Betsch Cole spoke on this theme in a talk titled, "The Social Value of Museums: Inspiring Change." She asserted the business case for diversity and inclusion, stating that "if businesses are to compete effectively in this global economy, they must have within their company, employees of diverse backgrounds who will bring different and innovative ideas to the table." She emphasized that "in the next thirty years, the US will become a majority-minority country with white folks no longer in the majority."[8]

Dr. Cole also reminded attendees that the future of philanthropic giving to museums is influenced by racial and ethnic diversity, and funders will prioritize efforts that have a positive effect on underrepresented populations. Considering the current rate of social and demographic change, developing comprehensive DEAI strategies will ensure financial stability and is also, undeniably, the right thing to do.

What you can do: While research on inclusion and sustainability in the private sector is plentiful, there is a great need for accurate benchmarking information and analysis about DEAI in the museum field. By highlighting DEAI successes at your museum, you can demonstrate that the work will benefit all.

Insight: Empowered, inclusive leadership is essential at all levels of an organization. Leaders are found at all levels of an organization. Your visitor experience team can, and should, be the champion of inclusivity and diversity for your organization.

Reflexively, people equate decision-making and culture-setting behavior with the C-suite, but frontline leaders not only directly affect the visitor experience, they also directly impact the day-to-day experience that staff has with one another, since frontline leaders interact with frontline employees all day, every day. Frontline leaders are the most visible role models, and they have significant power to either implement or ignore DEAI efforts. Additionally, trusting the understanding of less-senior, less well-paid, or temporary staff is a move that can provide incredible insight—insight that is often not found on the C-suite level.

What you can do: Visitor experience departments can prioritize inclusion through developing an inclusion plan.

- Highlight successes and reward team members for outstanding DEAI efforts and ideas.
- Provide training for new associates and emerging professionals.
- Establish resource groups for staff to learn more.
- Talk about it among the staff. Let them know that no idea is a bad one and that they are encouraged to share their thoughts, even if they challenge the norm.

Centralization of DEAI:
Your Visitors as Individuals with a Shared Humanity

We must face the reality that this can be a difficult topic. It's challenging because it forces some to do uncomfortable emotional work, but it's also tricky because even with the best of intentions, talking about it may feel intimidating. But there are specific initiatives that can be implemented in your visitor experience areas to make DEAI more central to operation.

Make DEAI initiatives a part of your visitor experience DNA.   Time and money will need to be invested in your DEAI strategy, but it's a long-term investment that has a healthy return. Regularly surveying experience staff on the progress of implemented initiatives, making DEAI a core element of staff evaluations, developing a formal visitor experience code of conduct, setting and tracking DEAI goals, and including structural elements that display a commitment to DEAI (lactation areas for staff and guests, gender-neutral bathrooms, etc.) are all things your museum can do to ingrain DEAI into your visitor experience culture.

Offer all frontline staff targeted training.   Museum visitor experience staff are often somewhat new to the field and are considered emerging professionals—they have received limited training in managing and coaching teams, even though their current positions require those skills.

A Boston Consulting Group survey[9] showed that the top 5 percent of companies in people development (including training programs across all levels) increase their revenue twice as fast as the bottom 5 percent of companies, and they increase their profits 1.4 times as quickly. To support visitor experience staff and maximize revenue, companies should offer continuous training on inclusion and provide formal training in spotting and overcoming unconscious biases, which all diverse groups in the study (women, people of color, and LGBTQ employees) ranked as one of the five most essential interventions for improving the DEAI climate. And bias training programs can't be a one-off—visitor experience sees too much turnover and promotion from within; instead, they need to become an ongoing, continuous part of a museum's career development path.

Make it a part of the daily routine.   Many of the negative experiences that underrepresented groups face at work are subtle rather than overt. Often, management isn't intentionally exclusive; they may not even be aware of how an incident or comment comes across. Because issues like this can be easily missed, inclusive practices and routines need to be a part of the daily routine.

In meetings or group discussions, leaders should ensure equal participation. Waiting for employees to contribute is often a situation in which majority groups typically feel more comfortable speaking up than underrepresented groups. Leaders should call on individuals by name and acknowledge everyone's ideas and input. They should track interruptions and rectify these situations whenever possible. For team projects, leaders should ensure that responsibilities and roles are equally dispersed so that people in underrepresented groups don't always bear the brunt of the work or feel like they have the more substandard positions on the team.

Support inclusive personnel decisions. Gut instinct is not an appropriate means of making personnel decisions—that is an approach that will reinforce existing biases. Instead, HR should seek out tools that help more inclusive and objective decision-making. Employee evaluations should reflect quantifiable criteria—not merely things like where employees are from, or their backgrounds and demographic attributes. Also, visitor experience leaders should receive training in how to provide specific, actionable feedback based on facts.

Seek out those who haven't felt welcome at your institution. Then invite them in.

Visitor Services Staff being Diverse, Inclusive, and Equal

In the article "We're Not That Hard to Find: Hiring Diverse Museum Staff"[10] author Joy Bailey-Bryant states: "Fostering museums' shift toward visitor-centric environments takes creativity and change; in turn, hiring diverse staff helps museums innovate and create, and ultimately changes the tenor of the stories we tell."

Once museums recognize the benefits of diversity and confirm their intention and commitment, they can take action. In a study conducted by the New York City Department of Cultural Affairs, 75 percent of organizations cited a lack of diverse candidates as a significant challenge.[11]

Strategies for identifying and developing various candidates can be adopted, which is especially crucial for the visitor experience department, because it typically has the highest percentage of turnover in museums, frequently interfaces with visitors, and has potentially the most opportunity to hire and recruit talent for a museum.

Hiring Diverse Candidates

Get existing staff on board and celebrate diversity that is already present. Invite diverse team members into the recruitment and hiring process.

Train leadership. With proper education, a frontline worker may become tomorrow's museum director. Empower those who enter the field with training, access to leadership, and opportunities for decision-making roles, because your frontline experience associate may be the next generation of museum leadership.

Whenever possible, offer paid internships over non-paid. Compensation equalizes people from all socioeconomic backgrounds and facilitates opportunities that might otherwise not be (literally and figuratively) afforded.

Foster mentorship. We want people from all walks to be with one another on an equal field because some commonalities that generally occur due to affiliations, like alma mater, family background, and membership in organizations, might not be as present when considering hiring, training, and promoting diverse staff. Communication and interaction between emerging professionals and those further in their careers helps balance perspective.

Form partnerships and relationships that will support diversification efforts. Many of your best hires will come from existing neighbors and friends.

Seek out pools of candidates. Organizations, such as Museum Hue, provide existing pools of diverse job seekers.

Even when hiring with the goal of diversity in mind, the efforts will not succeed unless museums create and sustain a more inclusive environment.

You can't always see an inequity or a disability, but colleagues and visitors will feel when one is perceived. These invisible barriers continually shadow, and can feel impossible to face silently, so the goal for your museum experience staff is to remove every possible barrier that could prevent a potential guest from visiting and, also, from having a good experience while there. Frontline museum staff is arguably the most influential museum staff on this ability. For many museums, the frontline staff is the most diverse, but they are, also, often the staff with the least amount of experience and professional training opportunities—further supporting why investment in their development is critical.

Accessibility

Museums, already faced with tight budgets and limited resources, would ideally be set up to serve any community that walks through their doors. So, while older museums or historic houses may not have been designed with accessibility in mind, and their resources may not be expansive enough to overhaul their entire physical spaces, there are things that frontline museum professionals can do, with the proper training, to enhance a museum's accessibility. Again, the pressure on frontline museum professionals is demonstrated in that they can make even an "inaccessible" museum, easier to navigate.

So, there are obviously different types of accessibility: physical access, financial access, and then more specific types of accessibility challenges for those in the deaf and hard of hearing community and those with autism spectrum disorders. For the purposes of this book, we are going to discuss ways front-of-house museum staff can have a positive effect on accessibility.

Empower your staff to understand. Accessibility work is about understanding the real and perceived barriers that make visitors feel unwelcome in museums. Frontline service staff must understand the needs of communities different from their own and learn to embrace experiences and meaning across a range of human abilities. Understanding disability and the way it functions as an identity is critical. "Disability" can be an umbrella term that applies to many different people. There are many types of disability, each community has its own culture and history, and each has different accessibility needs.

For museums, with such limited funding and staff resources, training to embrace this complexity seems overwhelming, but by taking the time to learn more about disability, museums can shape their understanding and interaction with disabilities and accessibility.

Accessibility is an action word. Frontline service staff, when properly trained, can be the natural people to start these conversations. Engaging as many diverse communities as possible in conversation is important to inclusion and access. Visitor services personnel should invite guest feedback on accessibility to ensure the broadest range of communities are being heard. If your actual visitors are not invited to provide feedback, then any accessibility changes or upgrades, while made with the best of intentions, would be based on assumptions, so this approach ensures that those people you are trying to reach are active participants in addressing the issues. Conversations around accessibility work best when both parties are equals working together to solve problems, so by asking questions and really listening to answers. An American Alliance of Museums article by Ryan Saglio, titled "Four Things I Learned When I Started Thinking about Museum Accessibility," hits on a key but often overlooked nuance: accessibility work isn't just about providing equal access, it's about equitable access. It's about making sure visitors have the resources to choose to experience the museum however they want.[12]

Access is not a burden.   Making your museum more accessible is not an encumbrance but an act of love for others.

Accessibility work doesn't have to be daunting—it's not a burden or a matter of ADA compliance; it is an evolving conversation. It involves committing to a community that is often forgotten and ignored. Accessibility done right doesn't just allow people to feel welcome; it instills a sense of belonging and gives them a place for their voices to be heard at your institution, paving the way for many others, for years to come.

Recommended Texts and Works

There is much to research and learn on the topic of DEAI. As Cecile Shermann, chair of the DivCom at the AAM, indicated in her article "A Totally Inclusive Museum," "Museums will never reach the goal of being fully inclusive because we will never be fully inclusive and would never be able to measure that on anyone's behalf."

If a driving resolution for museums is to enrich appreciation for cultural heritage and inspire beautiful growth and exploration within oneself, then museums cannot claim to be fulfilling their purpose until growth in the DEAI museum realm is attained and considered essential to a more whole society.

There are excellent articles, resources, and books written on this topic by our colleagues in (and outside of) the field, and the best thing we as museum professionals can do is continue to learn and grow from these texts and resources.

AAM and DEAI Resources

The American Alliance of Museums (AAM) website, Diversity, Equity, Accessibility, and Inclusion.

- https://www.aam-us.org/category/diversity-equity-inclusion-accessibility/
- https://www.aam-us.org/programs/diversity-equity-accessibility-and-inclusion/
- https://www.aam-us.org/programs/resource-library/diversity-equity-accessibility-and-inclusion-resources/ (resource page)

AAM Professional Network, Diversity Committee (DivCom)

Johnetta B. Cole and Laura Lott (AAM), *Diversity, Equity, Accessibility, and Inclusion in Museums* (Lanham, MD: Rowman & Littlefield, 2019)

Notes

1. Bailey-Bryant, Joy. "We're Not That Hard to Find: Hiring Diverse Museum Staff," *Museum* (American Alliance of Museums, January/February 2017). https://unitedarts.cc/wp-content/uploads/2017/05/were-not-that-hard-to-find.pdf.

2. Betsch Cole, Johnnetta, Laura L. Lott, Christine Anagnos, Dina Bailey, Brian Carter, Robert M. Davis, Eduardo Diaz, et al. "Facing Change: Insights from the American Alliance of Museums' Diversity, Equity, Accessibility, and Inclusion Working Group." American Alliance of Museums, April, 2018, 9. https://www.aam-us.org/wp-content/uploads/2018/04/AAM-DEAI-Working-Group-Full-Report-2018.pdf.

3. Garcia-Alonso, Jennifer, Matt Krentz, and Mai-Britt Poulsen. "It's Frontline Leaders Who Make or Break Progress on Diversity." Boston Consulting Group (BCG), bcg.com, March 5, 2020. Accessed May 3, 2020. https://www.bcg.com/it-it/publications/2020/frontline-leaders-make-break-progress-diversity.aspx.

4. Garcia-Alonso et al., "It's Frontline Leaders Who Make or Break Progress on Diversity."

5. Project Implicit. Accessed May 3, 2020. http://implicit.harvard.edu/implicit/.

6. "Museums as Economic Engines: A National Study." Commissioned by American Alliance of Museums. Conducted by Oxford Economics, December 2017. https://www.aam-us.org/wp-content/uploads/2018/04/American-Alliance-of-Museums-web.pdf.

7. Betsch Cole et al. "Facing Change."

8. Keynote address by Dr. Johnnetta Betsch Cole, 2015 American Alliance of Museums Annual Meeting, April 27, 2015. https://aamd.org/our-members/from-the-field/johnnetta-cole-museums-diversity-social-value.

9. Garcia-Alonso et al., "It's Frontline Leaders Who Make or Break Progress on Diversity."

10. Bailey-Bryant. "We're Not That Hard to Find."

11. Bailey-Bryant. "We're Not That Hard to Find."

12. Saglio, Ryan. "Four Things I Learned When I Started Thinking about Museum Accessibility." *Diversity, Equity, Accessibility, and Inclusion*, American Alliance of Museums, March 8, 2019. https://www.aam-us.org/2019/03/08/four-things-i-learned-when-i-started-thinking-about-museum-accessibility/.

4

The Experience Economy Approach, Applied in a Museum Setting

T HE EXPERIENCE ECONOMY APPROACH is an enduring business principle created by B. Joseph Pine II and James H. Gilmore in 1998 that is widely studied around the world. The application of the experience economy centers on forming unique connections to secure customer (in this case, visitor) affection and to ensure economic security. These "unique connections" come by way of offering a compelling experience, which, for museums, connects content with visitors and creates positive feelings around a visit. This chapter will focus on forming that connection in ways that frontline personnel can affect.

The Experience Concept

Businesses from all sectors have taken the specialty "experience" concept to extreme levels. Consider the "eatertainment" industry, which includes places like House of Blues, Rainforest Café, and Bubba Gump Shrimp Company. Diners don't necessarily seek these restaurants out for the cuisine but rather the experience of being immersed in their themes and interacting with their character-portraying staff.

Savvy "shoppertainment and entertailing" retailers have also adopted the experience economy philosophy. Many stores sell teddy bears, but at Build-a-Bear, the patron gets to build their own. The purchaser's experience of making their bear is why their newly built teddy bear costs three times the amount of an average bear. Many people that shop there may not have been in the market for a new teddy bear; instead, they were seeking an experience.

Through that experience, they have built a bear that will be associated with the time they spent at the Build-a-Bear store.

Physical retail stores are closing in unprecedented numbers. Chains that we grew up with as household names are going bankrupt, and shopping malls are closing. Companies like Instacart and Shipt, offering near-immediate delivery, make a trip into any physical store seem like a waste of precious time. Many stores that have been mainstays in the shopping mall scene—RadioShack, Sears, Sports Authority, Toys'R'Us, and Claire's Accessories, for example—are posthumously analyzed in business school case studies on the rise of online and app-based retailing. There is no incentive to visit a store when Amazon offers better prices, informative reviews, and fast delivery, with no need to leave your living room.

An article in the *World Economic Forum*'s Annual Report from 2019 asserts that the only companies that will exist in ten years are those that create and nurture human experiences. This learning and growth will come from maximizing opportunities, including the reinvention of retail spaces, new models of engagement, and an understanding of experiences as perhaps the most essential form of marketing.[1]

Retailers capitalizing on the experience are healthy. Lululemon builds community by offering free yoga classes in its stores. Bass Pro Shops, REI, Cabela's, and Patagonia are all sporting goods/outdoor retailers that focus on experiences—such as trips, indoor rock climbing, and outdoor sporting activities—as core parts of their business.

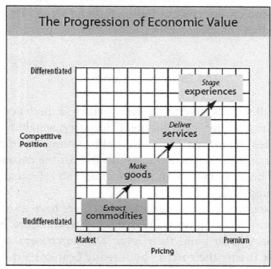

FIGURE 4.1
The progression of economic value.
Source: Pine II and Gilmore (2014).[2]

These experiential initiatives create emotional bonds between consumers and organizations and frequently have a higher return on investment through a more dedicated following than their digital counterparts. The brands that embrace the experience economy, and the data that powers it, are the ones that will survive.[3]

The experience economy philosophy suggests mixing in memorabilia,[4] which can be an integral part of any museum retail experience because some things are purchased primarily for the memories that they invoke. Vacationers buy magnets, keychains, and shot glasses to "remember" their trip, golfers purchase a shirt or cap with an embroidered logo to recall a course or round, and concert-goers obtain T-shirts with tour locations and dates on them. They are buying such memorabilia as physical reminders of experiences.

People spend tens of billions of dollars every year on memorabilia. These goods generally sell at price points far above those commanded by similar items that don't represent an experience. The price points are a function less of the cost of goods than of the value the buyer attaches to remembering the experience.

And experiences are not exclusively about entertainment; companies stage an experience whenever they engage customers in a personal, memorable way.

The Four Categories of Experience

Experiences are grouped into four broad categories according to where they fall along two dimensions.[5]

1. *Entertainment.* Watching television or attending a concert are those experiences in which customers participate more passively than actively; their connection with the event is more likely one of absorption than of immersion.
2. *Educational.* Educational experiences such as attending a class or taking a ski lesson tend to involve more active participation, but students (in this case, visitors) are still more outside the event than immersed in the action.
3. *Escapist.* Escapist experiences can teach just as well as an educational one can and can amuse just as well as entertainment, but they involve greater customer immersion. Acting in a play, playing in an orchestra, or descending the Grand Canyon include active participation and immersion in the experience.
4. *Esthetic.* Esthetic experiences have a minimal amount of active visitor participation. Here, customers or participants are immersed in an

activity or environment, but they have little or no effect on it—like a tourist who views the Grand Canyon from its rim.

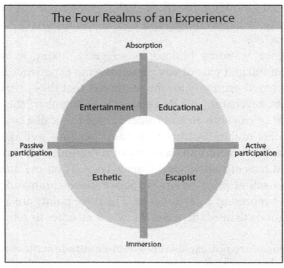

FIGURE 4.2
The four realms of an experience.
Source: Pine II and Gilmore (2014).[6]

The museum-going experience is exceptional in the way it spans these experience spectra. Interestingly, there are not many other industries that can claim this cross-section. It is a great benefit to the museum industry that the experience it offers can appeal to a broad range of experience seekers. The richest experiences possess aspects intersecting all four realms, forming a "sweet spot." Those working in the museum experience can ask themselves, "What specific experience will my museum offer?" The answer to that question may come to define their organization.

Like goods and services, experiences have to answer a customer need, they have to work, and they have to be deliverable.[7] Just as products and services result from an iterative process of research, design, and development, experiences derive from an iterative process of exploration, scripting, and staging.

The Museum as Theater and Being "On Stage"

The experience economy approach suggests the context of being "onstage"— and frontline staff as actors in a performance. Through exhibits, programs, and its people, a museum stages an experience—and the visitor views the total production. Everyone involved in the output has a dedicated role: the director is the museum's president, CEO, or executive director; the producer is the head curator; the production crew is the rest of the curatorial team; and the actors—the ones directly carrying out the rest of the team's vision and work—are the frontline staff. Everyone on the museum team has a role in the success of the production, and without everyone playing their parts, the production will fail.

Frontline Staff as Actors in Business Theater

Identifying frontline staff as the actors is more than fitting. Acting is the taking of deliberate steps to connect with an audience. It is not necessarily celebrity, Broadway, or sales, which may be some of the more generalized views of "actors." The latter runs the risk of exhibiting dishonest or fake roles that will provide little opportunity to engage visitors in new and exciting ways. There is a widespread opinion that acting isn't genuine, or that it is misrepresenting yourself, and bad acting is just that. But good acting is actually about doing less with more and presenting something to someone in a such a way that interacting with it will be desirable.

The smile, the warm welcome, making sure your guests know that you're here for anything they need during a visit—these are examples of impressions. Impressions are the takeaway of the experience and fulfill a theme. Experience stagers must eliminate anything that diminishes, contradicts, or distracts from the theme.

The experience economy likens this immersive experience to the now-world-famous example of the Pike Place Fish Market. Employees of the Pike Place Fish Market genuinely are fishmongers, and they act on their fish market stage—including the immortal image of workers tossing fish to one another.

ChartHouse Learning of Burnsville, Minnesota, illuminates four principles they use to create the Pike Place Fish Market experience in their *Fish!* video.[8] Each of its principles is an acting technique:

1. *Play.* While being a fishmonger may not be a traditional or mainstream career, the workers and customers are put on stage for everyone to enjoy being a part of the experience.
2. *Make their day.* The focus is on making sure the customers have a great experience, and to create lasting memories of their time spent there.
3. *Be there.* The workers cannot provide these experiences for customers if they are preoccupied, so one of their main mantras is to "Be Present" and enjoy the moments as much as the customers do.

4. *Choose your attitude.* Since acting is about making choices regarding what will connect you to your audience, there is a process of choosing which part of yourself to reveal to them. We act differently amongst our co-workers, old friends, neighbors, and family—and our characters change, though sometimes only slightly, to be modified to each audience. For example, you would act differently in front of your college roommate than you would in front of your grandmother.

Many workers fail to act, and when that occurs, they execute their work as though it is mundane, day-to-day activity. When workers act as though their job depends on it, they attain the engagement to which great actors aspire. The viewer connects, in that sought-after "unique way," to the actor and the production.

So, the museum experience staff can function as the actors or, maybe more appropriately "the connectors," but good acting is only one part of the full theatrical production. The stage also needs to be set for the visitor to believe and absorb an experience fully.

Staging the Experience

Staging the experience is about the details. It is about attending to the background needs so that the visitor can focus on having a consistent and positive experience.

Some critical elements of this process include:

1. *The script.* A foundational aspect of any excellent performance is a compelling and engaging script. Actors needn't follow a script word for word, but a good text can serve as the backbone for interaction. It helps to impart the organization's theme and serves as a valuable training tool to help new employees gain confidence. The scriptwriter can be someone with comprehensive experience at the museum. This might be the manager or director, someone who has experience with what visitors have wanted in the past and can use that knowledge to frame the script.
2. *Setting the stage.* Are things in the work area clean? Could your audience's attention be diverted by clutter, brochures, or personal items? Anything "off-theme" should be removed from sight to lessen the distractions. Experience stagers must eliminate anything that diminishes, contradicts, or distracts from the theme.

3. *Costuming.* Is the work attire appropriate to the experience? Is it fun and engaging? Serious and proper? It can be anything—as long as it cohesively supports your theme and doesn't distract from the overall production.

4. *The comfort of the viewing space.* Does the viewer feel comfortable in the area? Is it too hot or too cold? Is the lighting appropriate for the production? In a children's museum, it may be a brighter, fully lit atmosphere so that the children can interact with the hands-on activities, but in a glass museum, perhaps the lighting is dim, with up-lighting on the objects to highlight the details of the pieces. This, like the other elements, is entirely dependent on your theme and audience needs.

5. *The actors.* Are they sincere and believable? Do they convey the theme and impressions efficiently? With the guest experience staff at center stage, their training and behavior are central to the success of viewer believability and affection.

Getting into Character

Getting into character is a process all visitor experience staff must undertake before being in front of guests.

Character is essential for guest experience personnel because each one must be distinguishable; otherwise, you end up with an automated-sounding group of uninteresting clones. Take Barbra Streisand's audition for Harold Rowe's musical, *I Can Get It for You Wholesale*, for example. When she was a little-known actress, Streisand walked in late, wearing a flashy raccoon coat and mismatched shoes, loudly smacking (pretend) gum, and delivered a spellbinding performance with a very distinctive character. She got the part.[9]

This is not to suggest you should take this approach in your museum; however, knowing your character well and delivering it to your audience in a confident and unique way produces results.

The most thoroughly engaging people have perfect knowledge of their role and can perform it seamlessly, so that observers cannot tell they are viewing a performance.

Themes and Impressions

In theater, there are underlying themes that support the story. These themes drive the story and are backed by impressions, which are the takeaway of the experience. The actor supports the themes and provides the impressions.

There is a distinct threat in breaking character. Visitor experience professionals must behave in a manner consistent with the theme and the role the audience believes them to be, or there is a risk that the audience won't find the experience authentic.

The metaphor of a show is again quite fitting for frontline personnel because visitors do not want to see what is happening in the background of the museum experience—that would ruin the transcendental magic of taking in an exhibit. Visitors are watching the big picture, inclusive of details. All these things must be in alignment, as it's the fine-tuned, broad-view reality that viewers are evaluating as a part of their overall experience.

Fulfilling the Intention

With the intention in mind, the acting is fulfilled by giving the audience the basic facts and answers they are looking for. The underlying purpose of the actor in these cases is to enrich the museum-goers' experience and spark a desire to return, which leads to economic security. Visitors remember the well-executed experiences, and they also remember the terrible ones—they will not remember the middle-of-the road, mundane variety, so shoot for solid execution every time.

With that simple intention in mind, it is up to museum management to influence the script, set the stage, and give oversight to the costuming. Still, the execution of the experience remains entirely in the actor's hands. So, act! And deliver that flawless performance.

Notes

1. Yaffe, Jonathan, Andrew Moose, and Dana Marquardt. "The Experience Economy Is Booming, but It Must Benefit Everyone." *World Economic Forum*, weforum.org, January 7, 2019. https://www.weforum.org/agenda/2019/01/the-experience-economy-is-booming-but-it-must-benefit-everyone/.

2. Pine II, B. Joseph, and James H. Gilmore. "Welcome to the Experience Economy." *Harvard Business Review* (July-August 1998). Accessed August 1, 2014. https://hbr.org/1998/07/welcome-to-the-experience-economy.

3. Pine and Gilmore, "Welcome to the Experience Economy."

4. Pine and Gilmore, "Welcome to the Experience Economy."

5. Pine and Gilmore, "Welcome to the Experience Economy."

6. Pine and Gilmore, "Welcome to the Experience Economy."

7. Pine and Gilmore, "Welcome to the Experience Economy."

8. Pine II, B. Joseph, and James H. Gilmore. "Work Is Theatre." In *The Experience Economy: Work Is Theatre & Every Business a Stage*, second edition, 168. Boston, MA: Harvard Business Review Press, 2011.

9. Pine II and Gilmore. "Work Is Theatre," 153.

5

Magnetic Modeling and Dynamic Delivery

The Business of Museums

I N HER OPENING REMARKS from the 2019 Annual Meeting of the American Alliance of Museums,[1] president Laura Lott stated:

> Now, too often when I say that "changing business models for financial sustainability" is one of the Alliance's three focus areas, museum professionals politely nod and try to hide the glazed-over look in their eyes. . . . Too often, in my experience, there is a perceived division between those professionals who design the programs and curate the exhibits—and those who are responsible for maintaining the financial health of the institution. Sometimes our passion for the amazing work of museums blinds us to the business realities within our organizations and the disruptions and financial pressures coming from outside. . . . I fear that many of us are dangerously close to a fatal mistake of assuming that funding will come—somehow, somewhere—because we deserve it.

And museums do deserve it, but the formal recognizance that financial sustainability needs to be a key theme of museum operations is a refreshing perspective. That the governing Alliance for our field chose to make it the subject of their entire annual meeting is even more promising.

Despite sometimes being viewed as the least sexy department within a museum, visitor experience will inevitably influence a museum's financial security more than much else can.

Lott went on to urge conference attendees to take away two main ideas:

Museums will be better positioned to inform, inspire, and enrich our world if they have healthy balance sheets.

And,

Long-term financial sustainability is everyone's responsibility. And it's something we must talk about openly and honestly.

Museums of all sizes and themes are competing for the attention of visitors and their dollars, and the best way to win that attention is by offering an experience that is second to none.

Lott's call to action implored the museum field to innovate, experiment, and implement new business models to secure their financial futures. By putting those models in place, delivering those models successfully, and creating happiness and excitement around them, the revenue will follow. Lott left us with an indispensable piece of advice that day when she reminded us that "no money, means no mission."

The Model

There are many definitions of what a business model is, or should be, but Alexander Osterwalder, the author of the definitive handbook on business models, *Business Model Generation: A Handbook for Visionaries, Game Changers, and Challengers*, says a business model describes the rationale of how an organization creates, delivers, and captures value.[2]

What is your museum's business model? Do you have one? How do you create value for your visitors? And then how do you deliver on that value? Robust programs and exhibits are foundational, but the delivery of the experience can be enhanced by the people executing the delivery.

Your pizza shop may have the most delectable, authentic Italian pizza, made with sauce from freshly grown tomatoes, creamy mozzarella cheese, and a buttery crust that's baked to golden perfection; however, if the person who delivers that pizza to your customer's doorstep is late, rude, and uncaring, it doesn't matter how delicious your pizza is. That customer won't be back.

The Business Behind Museums

The money for museums has to come from somewhere, and museums have resourcefully developed many ways to derive income. They invariably require "for-profit-like" commercial activities to sustain themselves financially. Every museum's most effective funding mechanisms will be different, meaning one general universal museum business model won't work for all.

So, take the things you do well and find ways to do them better. For example, the Van Gogh Museum in Amsterdam capitalizes on its longstanding reputation of having a world-class staff and monetizing their knowledge and skill. Museum employees spend a great deal of time sharing their expertise in collections management practices with their corporate clients as a commercial revenue opportunity. Their ability to do this begins with their staff and the experience they can offer these clients.[3]

Fundraising, museum stores, cafés, educational programs, corporate sponsorships, event space rentals, and admissions are traditional ways your museum makes money. Since there must be margin to carry out a mission and each museum will experience different success rates with those various initiatives, it's essential to look at your balance sheet and see what has been making your museum money—and then maximize those efforts.

The initiatives listed above are influenced by the experience one has with your organization, rendering the experience being positive essential. So many times, we work and work to make a failing program succeed. We spend staff time, resources, and money trying to make a program or an exhibit popular, and sometimes the efforts just don't work. It is perfectly acceptable to walk away from an initiative if people aren't having a pleasant experience. Control what you can.

The Business Model Canvas is a visual framework to describe the different elements of how your museum works. It illustrates what the organization does, for and with whom it does what it does, and the resources it needs. It can be used to analyze your current model and display where you need work.[4]

One advantage of the Business Model Canvas is that it is not a linear description; it allows for needed changes in one area to be become clear and makes it easier to play around with improvements to current or potential models.

You can ask questions such as, "What would happen to costs or revenue income if we introduced new elements, programs, or exhibits?" This allows you to weigh effects and risks. It can also stimulate new ideas. "What if . . . ?" can be the most influential question when working with your Canvas.

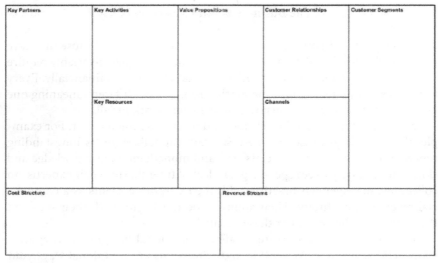

FIGURE 5.1
The Business Model Canvas
Source: Osterwalder and Pigneur (2010).[5]

The Museoprenuer Concept

In an article from the May/June 2019 issue of *Museum* magazine, Brendan Ciecko, CEO and founder of the museum engagement platform Cuseum, describes the museoprenuer as one who embraces or assumes characteristics of an entrepreneur to advance his or her museum's business model and general operations.[6] Museums adopting the museoprenuer approach are agile and able to act on the efficient parts of their business models.

Ciecko goes on to analyze the museoprenuer concept in practice—for instance, the New Museum in New York City founded its NEW INC initiative in 2014. It is the first "museum-led incubator" in the world and came of age at a time when shared office spaces were growing in popularity, especially in the tech sector. Members engage in a twelve-month program that places them into a "creative ecosystem," inventing new ideas and developing sustainable practices. The endeavor brings together more than one hundred entrepreneurs, artists, designers, and technologists in an eight-thousand-square-foot space, used as an office, workshop, social, and presentation arena. This opportunity for co-working and innovation is one way the New Museum saw an opportunity that would work for them and developed it.[7]

Visitor experience is one of the critical areas where business model capitalization can take place. Experiments in admission and membership can provide a significant return. When the Dallas Museum of Art (DMA) enacted its radical DMA Friends program, it offered free membership to its patrons. The DMA is among the ten largest museums in the country, and in 2013 they made a bold decision to enact a program where onsite visitors could sign up, for free, to be a "friend" (member) of the museum. They cited a desire to increase their understanding of individual participation in the museum and to collect in-depth audience demographics about who visits their museum—that was their need at the time. Any museum-goer could collect "badges" during a visit, and there was a reward system in place for the collection of these badges, such as a café discount and a late-night, private tour. The efforts culminated in allowing museum officials to see what did and didn't work in the museum, as well as which of their exhibits attracted the most visitors. The program was indeed an experiment and was discontinued in 2017, but the museum identified a need to support its model and attain the information they needed.[8]

Museopreneur Colleen Donnelly, a visitor experience professional with Boston Children's Museum from 2010 to 2019 and, most recently, chief of museum operations with Bailey-Matthews National Shell Museum, talks about a Five-Star Visitor Experience program she created while at the Boston Children's Museum:

> When I first arrived at Boston Children's Museum, the museum's CEO (who was also new to the museum) challenged me to improve visitor feedback, exhibit maintenance, and overall visitor experience. I began to read through online reviews, comment cards, and visitor emails. I also spoke to staff and visitors. During this time, I noticed common themes in what people were saying and what they wanted from their visit. They wanted great customer service, a clean and safe museum, exhibits that worked and had enough loose parts, engaging and fun programs, and easy access to the museum (i.e., affordable services for those with special needs). And from that, the idea of the Five-Star Visitor Experience program was born.

Donnelly describes the training and implementation process involved with instituting the program:

> This was not a small undertaking by any means. In reality, it meant that I would need to work with everyone in the museum to establish new procedures, pro-grams, and best methods. To begin, I ensured that all comments and feedback were thoughtfully addressed. I began the practice of personally writing to each visitor who reached out to the museum. I also worked with departments in the museum to address and remedy concerns in a timely manner. I pulled together

colleagues from the facilities, exhibits, and education teams to form a Five-Star committee. This team met weekly to discuss issues relating to the visitor experience and to develop and implement solutions. For larger concerns, we also included the CFO and the CEO. It is important to note that the Five-Star Visitor Experience program is not a checklist that is forgotten once all items are completed. Rather, it promotes ongoing evaluation of operations to ensure that the museum is consistently meeting the needs of current and future visitors. New employees receive Five-Star training, concepts from the program are communicated during all-staff meetings, and the program is now embedded in the museum's culture.

When asked about benefits the program brought to Boston Children's, Donnelly explained,

> The program was timely because, like in many organizations, different departments were working in silos. In addition, the main focus in terms of visitor experience was on customer service provided by the staff. When I read through their feedback and spoke with visitors in the museum, I realized that there was so much more involved in a museum experience and that every person and every department in the museum needed to be involved to make it work.

This program is on-going and will continue to evolve as visitors and their needs change. As museums, we encourage our visitors to be life-long learners. And, I believe that we, as museum professionals, must be as well. Change is hard and there will always be struggles, but it is important to stay focused on the goal of providing the best possible experiences for our visitors.

Some major initiatives that came about at Boston Children's Museum because of Five-Star include:

- a restructuring of the lobby to form an entry with a staffed greeter;
- an exhibit maintenance software program to report broken exhibits for immediate repair;
- the implementation of an EBT discount program for EBT card holders, the first in a Boston museum;
- weekly training for staff on child development, family engagement, and customer service;
- daily walk-throughs of all exhibits to check for safety, cleanliness, and functioning components;
- an exhibit mentor program which empowers floor staff and educators to look after exhibits and maintain loose parts; and
- the MorningStar access program, which invites children with special needs and their families to the museum at a time when no other visitors are present.

Donnelly concluded by saying,

> The Five-Star Visitor Experience program greatly improved daily operations at Boston Children's Museum. Visitor feedback ratings rose significantly, staff morale increased, exhibits were better maintained, program offerings improved, and the museum became more accessible. Five-Star brought together teams and departments and changed how the museum meets the needs of its visitors. I think the biggest take-away is that we all must all continue to listen to and talk with our visitors and each other in order to improve experiences. We cannot do it alone.

The Delivery

To sell your museum experience, you must know that you are the best person to get the job done.

In a *Harvard Business Review* article titled "The 5 Things All Great Salespeople Do,"[9] ideas are shared that even someone new to sales or who doesn't consider him- or herself a "salesperson" can implement. When considering the visitor experience, you are selling the visitors an enjoyable time. Visitors to a museum are not altogether buying a good or service. So, consider these tips to "sell" your experience the right way.

The best salespeople own it. Your success in making someone love something depends on you. Sales is a meritocracy—you see the same people repeatedly at the top of the sales and service leaderboard. These are the visitor experience professionals named in audience evaluation methods like Yelp and Trip Advisor, contributing to the excellence of a visit. They are the trainers when someone new joins the team. They are the team members who move into management roles.

These high performers could be cited as lucky, or as having an unfair advantage, but the most proven difference between top performers and everyone else is attitude. Approaching experience goals with an ownership mindset, is the mark of a quality experience professional. They control anything that happens to them. Psychologists have termed this way of thinking the "internal locus of control," a fancy way of saying that you believe the power lies inside of you, instead of externally. Having an internal locus of control corresponds with success in the workplace, higher income levels, and excellent health outcomes.

This ability seems to be deeply rooted in one's personality, so take a look around you and self-assess.

Take your current situation—your current role within your museum, the frequency of your promotions, raises and accolades, personal job satisfaction, and your earnings. Dig deeper on the path that you followed to get where you are. Ask yourself, Did I build the right connections and created a strong network? Did I work the nights, holidays, and weekends? Did I offer my ideas? Did I blame others for failures but take credit for the successes?

Notice the focus on yourself. In all of these questions, it's being asked if you completed the action. You must own the steps and their resulting outcomes. Within a museum, look at the experience within the galleries as if you can make it or break it. Walk your galleries every day and turn a keen eye toward the small details that can subtly shape a visit.

The best salespeople make it happen.   They don't bring problems, they bring solutions—good salespeople have a MacGyver-like attitude. MacGyver was the lead character from a show in the 1980s who was a nonviolent problem-solver who often concocted elaborate schemes to solve catastrophic situations. He didn't lament the job in front of him; instead, he assessed his strengths and resources and made something happen, and in every episode, he saved the day.

The best salespeople are MacGyver-like in their sales approach. Resourcefulness is a mindset as much as it is a skill. By starting with the MacGyver mindset, you can develop the skills associated with being resourceful.

So, embrace your inner MacGyver, and when a visitor brings an issue to you, fix it for them. If they mention they are hungry and ask for a recommendation for dinner, find out what flavors they are into, grab a map, show them the locations of your suggestions and then write down the address for them to take with them. You could even call and make them a reservation if needed. While this level of concierge service might not be typical in a museum, by adhering to it, you are ensuring they won't soon forget such a high level of commitment to their experience.

The best salespeople are experts.   Selling the experience is less about actual sales and more about leading, which requires high levels of confidence comprised of skill and learned knowledge—expressed mathematically: knowledge + experience = confidence to lead (and subsequently, sell). You can control the first part of this mathematical equation; the second part—gaining museum industry knowledge and a strong point of view about the value your museum can bring to your visitor's lives—takes some time.

Expertise leads to confidence, which leads to gaining visitor trust, which leads to a pleasant experience. Visitors feel at ease when they know that you know your stuff. You don't have to be an expert on your museum's theme, but be able to listen to their interests and provide them with suggestions on what they shouldn't miss during a visit.

The best salespeople help others.   You can teach someone something, no matter how far along you are in your career. There is something you know about the museum industry, your museum's theme, or your museum itself that someone new does not. The best salespeople regularly and altruistically pass their knowledge on to less-tenured or less-experienced salespeople, which in and of itself becomes a catalyst for building internal confidence.

Shawn Achor, the author of *Big Potential*,[10] found that social support providers at work ("work altruists") are 40 percent more likely to receive a promotion. The most authentic work altruists (those who provide the most support) are more than twenty times as likely as work isolators (those who offer the least social support at work) to make up for other employees' work in an effort to help them. Only 2 percent of work isolators help others with their work.

Further, only 5 percent of work isolators are extremely engaged in their jobs. Ninety-five percent of people who provide no social support at work have no work engagement. True work altruists are about ten times as likely to be highly engaged as work isolators.

More than half of true work altruists get along "extremely well" with co-workers. Only 20 percent of isolators get along exceptionally well with co-workers. Work altruists are twice as likely as work isolators to be satisfied with their jobs, and almost two-thirds of work altruists have excellent relations with supervisors.

All in all, being a work altruist wins, every time.

Many times, there is higher turnover in some of the more forward-facing museum positions, so use that as an opportunity to continually help your team learn new visitor experience strategies and tactics. The more you teach them, the better you will become at what you are teaching, so honestly, everyone wins.

The best salespeople move quickly.   The best salespeople have a sense of urgency. When I've encountered experience personnel who were slow in providing service, I have wondered if they even want my business. And since so many purchase decisions are spur of the moment, that instant of wonder has often made me second-guess if I want to be spending my time and money there.

If a museum visitor is asking you something, respond in a way that lets them know you value their time.

The Internal Locus

The locus of control is an individual's belief system regarding the causes and factors to which they attribute success or failure.[11] With an internal locus of control, you believe you have control over your efforts' outcomes.

You manifest your destiny. And if you want to see the things you do as successes, you will.

It's already been discussed that a key to success in knowing, sharing, and selling your museum is confidence, so it's no surprise that possessing an internal locus of control will equate to offering a more substantial experience.

Individuals with an internal locus of control—we'll call them "internals"—believe that it is up to them to succeed. "Externals" believe that fate or luck will more likely determine whether they will or will not become successful. Externals believe those circumstantial forces have more of an effect than the strength and quality of their efforts.

Psychologists argue that internals are born with this way of thinking, but it can also be developed. Some additional tactics to cultivate an internal locus of control include:

- Taking responsibility for things that happen in your life. The weight you give to things that happen to you is up to you.
- Responding mindfully to your emotions. Only you can upset you.
- Modeling your behavior and mindset after someone you recognize as being internally motivated. No one is responsible for how you feel except you.

As with many other areas in life, you can affect the museum experience with your attitude.

Exciting Your Visitors

Enthusiasm sells. When you are enthusiastic about your museum, your visitors will be, too. And that transfer of excitement is a pivotal point at which your visitors decide they are spending time in a place where they want to be.

Start where they are on the excitement meter. You don't want to annoy your visitors right out of the gate, but they need to feel the importance of your institution, why it's essential, and how exactly it contributes to their quality of life. You need to make them fall as much in love with your museum as you are.

In a 2014 McKinsey & Company sales insights article, titled "Can a Gold-fish Show You How to Excite Your Customers?,"[12] tactics were identified that for-profit businesses have employed to maximize excitement generation under their respective models:

They have made it simple. When visitors aren't bogged down with the words and the necessity to weed through intellectual and emotional clutter to have an experience, it becomes easier to have it. Take Amazon's one-click buying experience. It's the quickest and easiest online buying experience ever; no need to input your shipping address or fill in your credit card number. One-click, that's it. Visitors don't often want to be asked a million questions as they are purchasing their tickets. It's more comfortable for all involved to let the conversation evolve organically.

They have provided above and beyond service. Visitors will feel the love when exceptional service is offered. For instance, the UK floral company Interflora monitored the Twitter accounts of their followers and sent a bouquet to users who had expressed they were down. And just like that—Interflora created a customer for life. There is always something extra or unique you can do to put a memorable spin on the interaction.

They have cultivated hedonism. Provide fun, freedom, and shared experience—for example, the Burning Man festival. Burning Man is a week of community art, self-expression, and self-reliance. It has built a mass following of attendees who abandon modern-day life conveniences like money, cars, and cell phones to escape everyday life. People read novels, go to the theater or a movie, and visit a museum to escape their reality.

They have broken the norm. A more daring approach of rejecting stereotypes can have a significant impact. Instead of using professional models, the skin and hair care company Dove featured everyday women in its Campaign for Real Beauty, took a break from convention, which yielded Dove fifteen million viewers on YouTube. Museums can draw from this atypical approach. It's not always about being academic. Museums allow for teaching in a more tangible, fully absorbed manner. Let people learn the way they want, the way they learn best. Let them touch things. Let them be in areas traditionally off-limits or behind the scenes—"pull back the curtain." Make them usable for the everyday person.

They have formed co-creation opportunities. So many museums are allowing for visitor participation. There is a chapter that goes more in-depth on this later in this book, but by allowing for greater visitor engagement, there will be a greater connection to its content, which creates a better experience. Foster shared ownership through contribution and community. Social media has made co-creation an accessible way to excite customers. When Ford relaunched the Fiesta, it gave cars to a hundred social media influencers and asked them to write about the vehicle. The resulting blog provided customer-created content to fuel the Fiesta's popularity.

Excitement is not an accident, but it spurs from deliberate steps that leaders take to attract new customers and turn existing ones into lifelong supporters.

How to build excitement![13]

Drill down on your domain. Organizations cannot succeed at all of these ideas to excite, so select two or three directions that you want to own. What's your domain?

Generate ideas for breakthrough moments. Try "invention through transfer"—identify progressive ideas from other museums or places of learning and emulate them. Chart a course to deploy and track excitement ideas methodically.

Get your organization on board. Infuse excitement into your museum. Make it something you hang your hat on. Ensure leaders take strategic and symbolic action to support the change they want to see, whether it's by rewarding employees for contributing ideas on excitement or actually taking part in the exciting activities. What is the one thing you want your leaders to start doing?

Adopt a new philosophy of measurement. Excitement is explicitly disruptive, so it needs a new set of qualitative measuring tools to capture individuals' emotional impact. What metrics and tools should you be using?

Facilitate customer excitement, the next step in successful visitor experience. It offers you a chance to make your visitors loyal advocates for the experience your museum has to offer to your community.

Innovate, Experiment, and Implement Your Model

This is not a plea to concentrate on sales. By focusing on the delivery of the experience, sales will fall in step. By centering on a model tailored to a positive museum experience, delivering that model, and ensuring enjoyment and excitement surround it, the long-term financial sustainability that your museum deserves won't be far behind.

Notes

1. Lott, Laura. "Financial Sustainability Is Everyone's Responsibility." Opening general session of the 2019 American Alliance of Museums Annual Meeting, May 29, 2019. https://www.aam-us.org/2019/05/29/financial-sustainability-is-everyones -responsibility/.

2. Osterwalder, Alexander, and Yves Pigneur. "Preface." In *Business Model Generation: A Handbook for Visionaries, Game Changers, and Challengers* (Hoboken, NJ: Wiley, 2010), 14.

3. Ciecko, Brian. "Museopreneur: How Museums Are Leaping into New Business Models with an Entrepreneurial Spirit." *Financial Sustainability*, American Alliance of Museums (website), May 1, 2019. Accessed July 10, 2020, https://www.aam-us .org/2019/05/03/museopreneur-how-museums-are-leaping-into-new-business -models-with-entrepreneurial-spirit/.

4. Future Proof Museums. Business Model Canvas. Accessed July 10, 2020. https://www.a-m-a.co.uk/future-proof-museums-business-model-canvas/.

5. Osterwalder and Pigneur. "Preface," 14.

6. Ciecko, "Museopreneur."

7. Ciecko. "Museopreneur."

8. Ciecko. "Museopreneur."

9. Curtis, Joseph. "The 5 Things All Great Salespeople Do." *Harvard Business Review*, December 18, 2018. Accessed January 28, 2019. https://hbr.org/2018/12/the -5-things-all-great-salespeople-do.

10. Achor, Shawn. "What Giving Gets You at the Office." *Harvard Business Review*, July 27, 2014. https://hbr.org/2011/07/what-giving-gets-you-at-the-of.

11. Joelson, Richard B. "Locus of Control." *Psychology Today* (Sussex Publishers), August 2, 2017. https://www.psychologytoday.com/us/blog/moments-matter/ 201708/locus-control.

12. Hieronimus, Fabian. "Can a Goldfish Show You How to Excite Your Customers?" *Marketing & Sales*, McKinsey & Company (website), February 1, 2014. https:// www.mckinsey.com/business-functions/marketing-and-sales/our-insights/can-a -goldfish-show-you-how-to-excite-your-customers.

13. Bhattacharjee, Dilip, Jesus Moreno, and Francisco Ortega. "The Secret to Delighting Customers: Putting Employees First." *Operations*, McKinsey & Company, March 2, 2016. Accessed October 20, 2020. https://www.mckinsey.com/business-functions/operations/our-insights/the-secret-to-delighting-customers-putting-employees-first.

6

Onetime Visitors to Lifelong Friends

A N IMPORTANT THEME of the 2019 American Alliance of Museums (AAM) Annual Conference was financial sustainability, which got me thinking: for a museum, sustainability is perfectly embodied by a visitor becoming a member, staying a member for many years, and eventually becoming a donor. The notion that museums have a pipeline of giving that begins at the welcome desk begged exploration, and I decided to pitch a presentation session on this idea.

In brainstorming for the session, I realized I would need to bring in a marketing mind (and surprisingly, not a development one), because it wasn't so much the fundraising aspect of membership that I needed help with but rather the presentation and sales of it. So, my colleague Manny Leto, director of marketing and communications at the Tampa Bay History Center (TBHC), and I collaborated and presented a session titled "Onetime Visitors to Lifelong Friends."

The session was better received than we could have expected; every chair was full.

It seemed this was a topic many museum professionals were interested in investigating and stemmed the idea for this text. If that many museum professionals were interested in examining the critical role that frontline experience staff can play in a museum's success, then it should be addressed. So, this chapter will cover the following:

- Merging membership staff and visitor services to create a cohesive experience department.

- The role a good experience plays in a visitor joining as a member.
- Moving the front-desk focus from the museum's topic toward sales. Visitor services staff are often aspiring curators rather than aspiring guest experience agents.
- The lack of organizational focus on membership and visitor services.
- Tracking sales and performance-based scheduling.
- The philosophy of the membership program: making it a whole experience and not just an annual pass. Members are a part of your community.
- Ensuring your membership is inclusive and reflective of all visitors.

Merging Membership and Visitor Services

In 2015, after six steady years of declining membership numbers, the TBHC decided to make a change. The AAM's 2015 Annual Conference in Atlanta, Georgia, had featured a session on the importance of membership acquisition taking place at the visitor services desk. I remember thinking, "It makes sense. The most likely time for someone to purchase a membership to an organization or attraction is right after they have had a great visit there, want to return soon, and want to support what they saw."

The visitor-to-member conversion should feel natural. If you create an atmosphere and brand where people want to spend time and have quality impassioned people representing it, it's easy to imagine people wanting to become a part of that community.

The month after we returned to Tampa from the conference, the decision was made for TBHC to move membership under the visitor services umbrella. The benefits were apparent almost immediately:

1. The person directing the department was able to have a full picture of who was delivering because both metrics—visitor experience and membership sales—now fell under their purview; they drove both in a complementary and consistent way.
2. The people selling membership were extremely well-versed on the benefits of membership and were invested in the membership fund; equally, they were concerned about the visitor experience being positive. They knew a membership sale would hinge on the experience the visitor had.
3. The visitor experience and the member experience became organically entwined. Frontline guest experience staff became more comfortable

and displayed pride in ownership when discussing the potential experience a visitor could have once becoming a member.

In sum, both the membership and the visitor experience were greatly enhanced by the merge.

Good Experience = Your Next Member

The number one most useful strategy we have employed since converting into one big, happy department is offering visitors a chance to apply what they paid that day toward a yearlong membership—an opportunity to join the community they have just experienced firsthand.

Museums continually evolve to meet the demands for which today's society looks in the places they spend their precious free time, aiming to offer their visitors a safe, clean, intellectually stimulating place where they can be a part of a diverse community that is offering fresh, fun, and educational experiences.

It is a continual evolution. In 2018, a *Forbes* magazine study[1] indicated that 89 percent of companies compete primarily based on customer experience—up from just 36 percent in 2010. Further, 80 percent of companies believe they deliver a superior experience; but only 8 percent of customers agree, which is good news to those reading this book because you have already identified that the museum guest experience is all-important and are moving in the right direction. Everything a museum does—the way it plans exhibits, its marketing, it personnel training, and more—all play a role in shaping the visitor experience. Focusing on guest experience management may be the most influential investment an organization can make.

As mentioned, having a positive experience during a museum visit is a critical step in the visitor deciding to become a member. This idea furthers the point that to drive financial sustainability at your organization, you must provide that world-class experience. Your museum's balance sheet depends on it.

From a purely economic standpoint, when applying the cost of a visit toward a membership—meaning, when a visitor only needs to pay a small additional sum beyond the entrance fee to become a member—the decision to become a member becomes simple. This allows the visitor both the value of what was experienced during the visit, plus the positive feelings of joining a community and supporting a cause.

Guest Point of View

So, what makes for a positive experience? How can we define a universal "good time"? Experience is, in essence, intangible, so how can its success be measured? An article, "A Conceptual Model of Service Quality and Its Implications for Future Research,"[2] by Parasuraman, Zeithaml, and Berry, published in 1985, lists what these authors and service experts believe to be the ten determinants of service quality, and has served as an expert guide for the last thirty-five years. Their appointed determinants are:

1. *Reliability*: the organization is consistent and keeps its promises.
2. *Responsiveness*: the staff is ready and willing to provide timely service.
3. *Competence*: the staff possess the required skills and knowledge to successfully perform the service.
4. *Access*: the service is approachable and easy to obtain.
5. *Courtesy*: all contact personnel are polite, respectful, considerate, and friendly.
6. *Communication*: visitors are informed in a way they understand and are carefully listened to.
7. *Credibility*: the organization and its staff are trustworthy, honest, and believable, and have the visitors' best interests at heart.
8. *Security*: the experience with/at an organization is free from danger, risk, or doubt.
9. *Understanding*: efforts are made to meet the visitor's needs.
10. *Tangibles*: there is physical evidence of the service, including the physical facility and any other physical representations of the service.

Of note, these all deal with the perception of the visitor, or their point of view. Service, interaction, and experience that fails to meet these ten key determinants means that there will be a gap between the visitors' expectations of what should be and what the museum is actually providing. This comparison of expectations with performance is illustrated in their Service Quality Model. Also illustrated here are the "gaps" between the elements of service delivery, which can result in a negative experience.

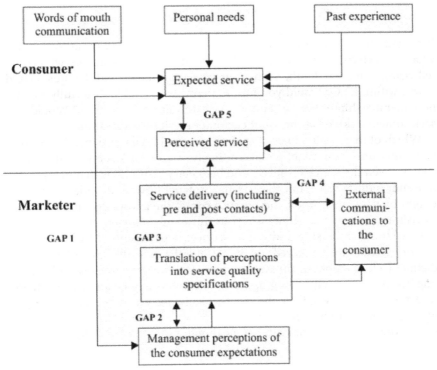

FIGURE 6.1
The Service Quality Model
Source: Parasuraman, Zeithaml, and Berry (2021)[3]

For more on visitors' common needs, written from a visitor's point of view, the 1996 document titled the "Visitors' Bill of Rights," originally published in *Curator: A Museum Journal* and written by Judy Rand,[4] is a great resource. The "Visitors' Bill of Rights" speaks to visitors' need for comfort, caring, and acceptance and seeks to break down barriers to our museums—in order to offer better physical, intellectual, emotional, social, and cultural access—all from the visitor's first-person point of view. It may be surprising, what a simple walk-through of museum galleries, from the guest's perspective, can unveil.

The Front-Desk Focus

If considering hiring someone to sell memberships for an organization, for what characteristics would you look? Would you want someone who could tell visitors, in great depth, about your museum's theme and the most prized works within it? Or would you hire someone who could masterfully express how membership to the museum would add value to their lives? Would you seek someone skilled at the art of customer service conversation?

Which of these individuals, do you think, would sell more memberships to your museum? You might feel it's difficult to hire someone with this proficiency, given the scarce resources and budgetary restrictions that many in the museum industry face, but these traits are taught by good leaders. They are taught by you! With study and practice comes the knowledge of how to talk to visitors in a way that showcases your museum's value points.

Once the membership and visitor services departments at the Tampa Bay History Center were merged, there was a realization that there had been a distinct lack of emphasis on sales training and tracking. We realized that no one had been carefully managing the membership acquisition process; therefore, sales were missed. Even the idea that someone was now on the front line, paying attention to how many conversions were taking place, was enough to propel the front line to offer it in a meaningful way to each visitor.

Organizational Focus

Historically, a museum's focus is on its collections and programs, not on selling tickets and building up membership. But the irony is that when you focus on the latter, you can do the former better.

In 2015, when the TBHC decided to merge the departments, we moved our focus and put some resources behind a sustainable model. Then, we had a newly formed membership and visitor services department—hence, the birth of our experience department, which was actually a little scary in its novelty.

The first thing we did was reorganize the management. We created a manager and an assistant manager role, with each person having a different concentration. The manager's purpose was to ensure customer service excellence and operational efficiency. The assistant manager's purpose was to ensure a smooth visitor-to-member transition and reliable data management to inform who was coming and subsequently joining. Soon, we had the visitor side and the member side, and they both reported to me, the newly titled director of experience.

Our re-organization complete, we recognized our failing numbers and the high hopes of the executive staff and then decided what to do next.

Step-by-Step

We realized we needed to change the department's motivation. We had to get the frontline staff excited about converting members. We found the number one way to do so was to let them see that more members would add value to their lives personally, which we achieved through performance-based scheduling: no sales quotas, no incentives. If you are fulfilling the action of offering membership to every visitor, you will receive scheduling preference. It didn't matter the length of tenure or academic credentials. The only thing that mattered was performance.

We also did not focus on competition. Sure, a little competition keeps everyone sharp, but you are building a team—and a team works together, not against one another.

The Philosophy of Your Membership

The philosophy of the membership program became one of community. We felt like we were building a more abundant, interconnected family—all who cared deeply for Florida's history (and yes, I know what you are thinking: Florida has history?). That members get annual pass related benefits to your museum is a harmonizing plus, but an authentic benefit of a membership is becoming a part of the museum's community and adding value to its members' lives.

The social aspect of membership, feeling like you belong to something and like you have a space to share with people who have the same values as you, is powerful. Members automatically have something in common with one another. It's not uncommon to watch members befriend one another—senior adult learners there for a morning lecture, young families on a Saturday morning by the hands-on train table, and so on. It's rewarding when you realize that you have fulfilled a need for these visitors beyond education. You have enriched their lives in more ways than one.

When you aren't selling them a "thing," it's hard to conceptualize what you are offering, but it culminates in the full, enriched experience.

In a 2018 National Awareness, Attitudes, and Usage study[5] (NAAU) on which benefits drive membership sales, one hundred and eight thousand individuals in the US were surveyed on their perceptions and behaviors regarding exhibit-based organizations such as museums, botanical gardens, historic sites, science centers, aquariums, and zoos. Participants were members (paying less than $250 annually) to these exhibit-based cultural organizations, and were asked about their opinions on their membership's most important benefits.

The study found the most desirable benefits were: free admission, invitations to member events, guest passes, and supporting the organization's mission to be the most significant motivators when making a membership purchase.

This data is vital because it shows potential members are looking for enriching experiences for their lives. Lesser-valued member benefits include free parking, tax deductions, and member newsletter communications—so, non-experience-based benefits.

An Inclusive and Reflective Membership

Too often in the membership world, I have heard that someone "looks" like someone who might join the museum as a member.

No one looks like they might join as a member. Everyone is a possible member.

I can't say that loudly enough. Everyone is a potential member, and every visitor who visits your museum should be offered the opportunity to become a part of it. By offering membership to every visitor, you are not only combatting the bias mentioned in chapter 3, you are building a group that is truly reflective of your diverse community.

As an additional plus, statistically, the more visitors that are offered membership, the more visitors that will join. Visitors who haven't visited very many museums may not be aware that a membership program exists. Visitors can get so caught up in their experience of a visit that they may not be thinking about membership.

There is no downside to making it a rule, without exception, that every group of visitors must have the word *membership* mentioned to them during a visit.

The Pipeline of Giving

As a result, the TBHC started to see growth. Three years post-merge, the center saw an approximated 46 percent increase in overall membership revenue. By three years after the restructure, the number of membership households had doubled and by five years later they had tripled. As a result, programs, lectures, and camps had more attendees, the mailing list for marketing efforts had expanded, and members could be extended asks for other ways to support the museum. Building up a committed membership base—a base that will support the museum through hard times, celebrate the museum's wins, and bring their friends and family to get them involved, too—is a strategy mostly dependent on museum experience staff. The pipeline of giving that can begin at a welcome desk, or from that first interaction, is a critical part of long-term financial sustainability strategy.

Notes

1. Hyken, Shep. "Customer Experience Is The New Brand." *Forbes*, July 15, 2018. https://www.forbes.com/sites/shephyken/2018/07/15/customer-experience-is-the-new-brand/.

2. Parasuraman, A., Valarie A. Zeithaml, and Leonard L. Berry. "A Conceptual Model of Service Quality and Its Implications for Future Research." *Journal of Marketing* 49, no. 4 (1985): 41–50. doi:10.2307/1251430. https://www.jstor.org/stable/1251430.

3. Parasuraman, Zeithaml, and Berry. "A Conceptual Model of Service Quality and Its Implications for Future Research."

4. Rand, Judy. "The 227-Mile Museum, or a Visitors' Bill of Rights." *Curator: The Museum Journal* 44, no. 1 (January 2010): 7–14. https://doi.org/10.1111/j.2151-6952.2001.tb00024.x.

5. Dilenschneider, Colleen. "What Are The Most Important Membership Benefits? (DATA)." Colleen Dilenschneider: Know Your Bone, July 25, 2018. https://www.colleendilen.com/2018/07/25/important-membership-benefits-data/.

7

The Curators of Experience

ENGAGEMENT REQUIRES THE INTENTIONAL giving of one's *attention*, unselfishly, to someone or something else. As French philosopher Simone Weil says in her classic *Gravity and Grace*, "Attention is the rarest and purest form of generosity."[1] She describes how attention is the contemplative practice through which we can reap the most profound rewards of our humanity.

About attention, Mary Oliver, one of our era's most prolific poets, writes: "Attention without feeling is only a report."[2] And cognitive scientist Alexandra Horowitz says: "To fully feel life course through us, indeed, we ought to befriend our own attention, that intentional, unapologetic discriminator."[3]

This chapter is on museum engagement, and while participation is a different concept than museum experience, the two are uniquely intertwined.

Most museum engagement efforts center on creating appealing programming and a deepening of the museum's connection to the community through its collections and exhibits. So, philosophically, to have the experience, you must have engagement, and how one interacts with the other begs exploration.

Engagement is the act of thinking and feeling. Experience is the act or process of directly perceiving events or reality. There is a very moment of engagement; it is when one's attention and interest are being held. Experience has a decidedly past-tense connotation in that there's no single "point" where it happens. It's the overall feelings of perception you have about time spent.

Engagement can be tricky because you can't make someone be engaged.[4] It has to come from within one's self. Someone engages with something (or someone) when they find the content (or person) exciting and accessible.

In a museum setting, the experience runs parallel to engagement because the overall experience will be shaped by several points of engagement, both with its objects and with its people. Experience is the fact or state of having been affected by, or gained knowledge through, direct observation or participation in these engagements.

You might say engagement deals with psychology and even neurology, which is why it helps to clearly define experience, because where engagement can be abstract, experience is the concrete act and process of directly perceiving events or reality.

In this chapter, we will discuss the importance of guest engagement, look at the ways engagement and experience are entwined, and explore why the success of one hinges on the success of the other. We will also talk about ways in which guest experience architects can enhance the engagement experience.

The Importance of Museum Engagement

Museum engagement is all-encompassing. Everything the museum does is to actively engage visitors, and the topic of engagement is popular amongst museum professionals. The millennial generation, digital platforms, interactivity—innovative ways to engage with a museum are endless. In *Magnetic: The Art and Science of Engagement*, Anne Bergeron and Beth Tuttle delineate that engagement is both an art and a science.[5]

Engagement is an action word that conjures up a brain image of being propelled forward with power and energy.

Engaged museums thrive on connecting people with the subjects and ideas housed within them. Engaging museums do this and focus on creating meaningful experiences that have emotional resonance, which creates a fulfilling visitor + museum experience. Additionally, they engage internal audiences, like their staff, plus the communities they serve.

Museum engagement in application involves a 360° approach. Participatory museums engage in a variety of ways on-site and virtually, and they have embraced their service to the public. They commit the entirety of their resources to meet the needs of the people they serve.

Engagement becomes a pillar of a museum's existence.

Then there is the scientific part; in *Magnetic*, Bergeron and Tuttle liken the science of engagement to a real magnet and its inner workings. Electrons circle a nucleus of atoms, which creates an electrical current. The current moves the particles. And when the atoms' currents align, a magnet is formed. Naturally, if those atoms ever become misaligned, they become demagnetized.

They go on to say that this is also how engagement works—reinforcing both the 360° nature of a magnet but also the movement described earlier.

In short, when the core vision of a museum aligns with its staff, volunteers, board, audience, donors, peers, and partners, the science of engagement can be achieved.

So, you know the art and science of achieving it, but we go back to the aim of defining what "it" is.

Engagement is the act of holding someone's interest and attention. In Nina Simon's *The Participatory Museum*,[6] she uses words such as "collaborating," "creating," and, of course, "participating" interchangeably with the word "engaging." She gives an overview of how a visitor can be an active participant in their museum visit.

She has a chapter in the text titled "Participation Begins with Me," the theme of which focuses on frontline staff being the "personalizers" of a museum visit. She notes that museums, as institutions, can establish deep relationships with small subsets of visitors: donors, researchers, and community partners, but that these niche groups are small and not a cross-section of regular, everyday visitors. Meaningful relationships with visitors are possible but the model needs to demand less resources and to be quick and easy to enact. There are many reasons why these meaningful relationships are essential, such as a deeper connection to the institution's theme and mission, and they mostly serve the museum's bottom line.

When it's perceptible to visitors that a responsive frontline staff exceeds their needs—they will be more likely to return, join as members, and pass around positive word of mouth. Simon mentions that frontline staff are active relationship brokers. Security guards, greeters, and museum store staff are the personnel who will have the most intimate knowledge of visitor needs. They are a "public face" of an institution, and as such, you want their purpose to be so much more than to answer directional questions and to remind visitors that no food or drink is permitted; you want them to be the facilitators of connection—the curators of experience.

I spent twelve years as a server. Waiting tables was how I put myself through college, but it's also how I formed my social connections and fine-tuned my hopes and dreams. Serving taught me a lot of lessons, but how to engage the diner was perhaps one of the most important. Diners can have dinner at any number of restaurants; why should they choose yours? I learned that it's not about taking their orders and bringing them their food and drinks. It's about facilitating an experience that will take them away from their norm; they don't need to do the dishes, it feels luxurious. In a perfect world, dinner is served by someone who wants to be serving it and who wants to make these precious moments pleasant for the diner by providing scarcely available, much sought-after attention.

When I began my tenure in museums, I continued to wait tables at night for several years even after I went full-time, because I was honing my skills. I was beginning to realize that the museum business, actually almost all business, is in the business of people. It is widely known that museums add value to people's lives; museums are culturally and educationally significant, and I love to get lost in a museum for all of the same reasons that my diners loved to eat at the steakhouse where I worked.

Experiencing a museum can be like reading a good book; you can forget the laundry mound on your sofa or the sink full of dishes. As long as the engagement is active and, as a visitor, you commit to the participation, you can lose yourself.

An example Simon gives as an effective way of "participating" is at the Apartheid Museum in Johannesburg.[7] Here they frame the entire museum experience by having you enter the museum through a "two doors" device that separates visitors and forces them to enter via two different paths based on whether they identified as white or non-white, intentionally profiling visitors to spur frustration and discussion. It is a provocative way to have a museum visitor participate, but it is effective at alienating visitors to invoke an emotional response. This example illustrates the engagement vs. experience concept. By visitors engaging with the entrance element at the Apartheid, it sets the tone and pace for the experience.

Patrick Wittwer, a professor of visitor experience in cultural institutions, a longtime manager of the Wells Fargo Museums, and the current marketing and communications chairperson of VEX (Visitor Experience Group), describes a program in which the visitor experience staff—who are, at the Wells Fargo Museums, named museum assistants—can directly affect the connection through their open-ended questions initiative:

> At the Wells Fargo Museums, many of our museums assistants were recent graduates of public history or museum studies master's programs. On paper, their role was to staff the front desk and give tours to guests. They were giving guided, lecture-based tours of a one-room museum, and after some reflection, I realized that interactive, discussion-based activities would convey the same information in the more engaging format of open-ended questions, or, questions that require a bit of thought and an extended answer—not a "yes" or "no" or "true" or "false." They are intended to encourage discussion between the person delivering content and their audience. The need to switch to this model came from observing tours early on in my tenure. Visitors were reticent to stay for a full tour, and I ended up asking the team to give me a tour so I could experience it from beginning to end. This led to me finding that even the most engaging

presenter wasn't able to hold my interest for the duration of the tour and I was [obviously] fully invested in the topic. I imagined what it would be like for a visitor with little to no interest in the topic and knew we had to find a new way to present this information.

When asked about the initiative's implementation, Wittwer replies,

The program arose organically—I have an uncommon "Let's get out on the floor and see how it works!" approach, and my team adapted quickly. One of the first programs we beta tested was a play-based activity that compared the stagecoach to modern methods of transportation. Using guided play with a few toys, we were able to illustrate the evolution of money-moving and people-moving technology from the 1850s to modern times, make meaningful connections between our visitors' everyday experiences and our story, and center the visitors in our content delivery.

Wittwer goes on to provide more examples of the initiative:

Our tours always began at a map of the United States from 1852. Originally, the museum assistant would point out our location on the map, the location of the Gold Rush, and differences in the map between 1852 and today. When we adjusted our content delivery, we moved from telling them what they are looking at to asking them what they are looking at. What is this a map of? Does it look different to you? Where do you think we are on this map? Where do you think the Gold Rush happened? How would you get from here to there? What's the best way to travel from here to there? . . . We found this interactive approach effective, as evidenced by a growth in visitation and a difference in our student groups. I liked to ask questions at the end of a group visit to see what, if any, information was retained. Getting answers to these questions after a lecture-based tour was excruciating. After an inquiry-based experience, students were eager to share what they learned and clearly retained more. Essentially, the lesson taken away from this whole experience was that if you, as a deliverer of content, not only involve but center your audience in the content delivery, it will make a longer-lasting and more meaningful impact.

The Ways Engagement and Experience Are Entwined

Once the Cooper Hewitt, Smithsonian Design Museum in New York City reopened in December of 2014, after a three-year renovation, visitors found the museum had been redesigned to take engagement to the next level. There were touch-screen tables that facilitated collection searches by color, motif, or shape. There was an immersion room that displayed the museum's vast collection of wallpaper projected on the wall and then allowed the visitors to design their creation. They even came up with something called "the Pen," which was a two-sided instrument—on one side a nib for drawing and on the other an NFC (near field communication) reader—that visitors checked out at the beginning of a visit. Visitors could draw on touch screens throughout the galleries and save the drawings with a touch of the NFC throughout their tour.

When the Pen was returned, the visitors were able to retrieve their "curated collections." The illustrated point here is that "the Pen" turned the passive observer at the Cooper Hewitt into an active participant.[8] Throughout this text, we have spoken about how a museum's people are the architects of experience within museums. Still, these types of active engagements with things, like in the case of the Cooper Hewitt, Smithsonian Design Museum, play a vital role in the museum experience, as well. The full museum experience marries the interaction with its people to the people's interaction with the objects and exhibits.

A Case Study in Experience Curation: The Institute of Contemporary Art / Boston

In 2010 at the Institute of Contemporary Art / Boston (ICA), then assistant director of education and visitor experience and current audience engagement chairperson of VEX, Krista Dahl Kusuma, had a vision for a newly created visitor experience program:

> As the ICA was growing into its new space and was rapidly evolving, the opportunity to reimagine the gallery staff arose. I developed a vision for visitor engagement in this new ICA: one that puts the emphasis on the visitors, not just on the works of art themselves. To make this model effective, gallery staff was reimagined. Taking advantage of this opportunity, I pioneered the highly acclaimed and widely duplicated Visitor Experience program at the ICA. The Visitor Experience program was designed and regularly retooled to be responsive to an inclusive public.

Kusuma lists the two key innovations, central to the program:

> First, how they perform their work. The gallery staff has to be approachable and adaptable; able to proactively engage and tailor the experience to the visitors' expectations and diverse backgrounds. Second, how we recruit and train them. We train staff and volunteers to be especially sensitive to urban youth, people with special needs, and the traditionally underserved and vulnerable in our community.

Kusuma continues,

> The Visitor Experience program aims to provide guests with an optimal visit experience and ensures that guests, including those from our target audiences, enjoy uniquely tailored engagement. The cornerstone of this program is the team of forty-plus visitor assistants (VAs) who are educators but also hybrid customer service specialists and proactive "safe-guarders" (i.e., as opposed to reactive security guards). VAs are so called because they exist primarily to advocate for and serve the visitor. Many of the VAs are practicing artists and/or art students; all offer guests a personalized encounter with art that is nuanced, engaging, and thoughtful.

When asked how the need for the Visitor Experience program was recognized, Kusuma replies,

> The conventional museum engagement framework compartmentalizes specialized functions, none of which prioritizes the visitor's experience. For example, security guards are tasked with guarding works of art. Docents give lectures to a captive audience and are only available at predetermined times. Visitor services offers guests a friendly face at admissions, but they may not be accessible to guests after check-in, and their ability to deliver content varies considerably. Visitors are then forced to rely on signage or worse, electronic devices, to guide them. We recognized that all this had to change to a more inclusive, synergistic system. In turn, this required the buy-in of all departments.

She stresses,

> To make this change, it is important to understand that the program lies at the intersection of multiple departments, especially curatorial and security. Each department was acutely aware that the Visitor Experience program was a viable solution to address their collective needs. The gallery staff enabled curatorial to develop exhibitions that were increasingly ambitious and complex in material, display, and content. VAs, by their presence and training, helped ensure that the guests and the work remained safe; a benefit that assuaged security's concerns. Further, both curatorial and education wanted to minimize the use of traditional museum barriers, like cases and stanchions around artworks, which gave guests the feeling of greater access, while also increasing the level of risk. Again, it was the VA that presented as the best solution for ensuring guests continued to enjoy access to the works.

Kusuma notes, she was at the right place at the right time to be able to introduce these changes:

> As the ICA was just coming into its new space and growing its staff, I was able to direct the vision by rewriting the playbook; new job descriptions and staff train-

ing helped me create and rapidly scale a team with a visitor-first focus. Staff were hired and held to high professional standards, and over time they earned—and were treated with—the respect of peers across the organization.

The need for an adaptable organizational flow is highlighted in the way the program was instituted. Kusuma details,

> The most significant shift was in the preparation of the gallery staff. Now redefined as members of the education department, the visitor assistants were specially trained to serve guests as skilled educators and facilitators. We assiduously trained our staff to be approachable and proactively-but-politely engage—a dance that required considerable preparation and finesse. Further, we rejected the notion that engagement is a one-size-fits-all approach and we gave our staff the tools to tailor the experience and match their delivery to the expectation of a diverse audience. And this is also why I had to significantly increase the diversity and qualifications of the hires.

From the very start of each shift, the focus is on experience:

> All staff reporting for duty began their shift in a mandatory, paid morning meeting led by one of the gallery supervisors, a VA lead, or me. This meeting time was, in practice, a focused, strategic spot-training designed to enhance engagement and troubleshoot issues that arose. The morning meeting calendar offered different topics daily; each was devised to address a customer service, safeguarding, and/or education imperative. In addition to the daily training program, we offered gallery educators paid curator- and educator-led trainings on new exhibitions, as well as a position in rotation during install that afforded staff paid and dedicated study time.

Kusuma notes,

> Over time I worked to mentor and empower the VAs to take responsibility for their team's development. With this in mind, the VA lead role was created as a step between visitor assistant and gallery supervisor; and I worked with the supervisors to identify, promote, and prepare this cadre. VA leads led morning meetings, gathered visitor feedback, managed the floor in the supervisors' absence, and were instrumental to new staff onboarding. Plus, they were a valuable bridge between the VAs, who regarded them as respected peers, and their managers. And they helped close the gap for staff who may have missed a morning meeting or other training.
>
> An important achievement we secured for the Visitor Experience program was the development of a tiered pay schedule, which gave staff access to raises well before their one-year work anniversary. Front-of-house staff are traditionally compensated poorly in organizations across the country. We wanted to

create a system of more competitive pay, plus appropriate compensation for tenure and exemplary performance. This pay schedule was an important step in stemming high turnover and cultivating staff loyalty. Lastly, it goes without saying that a staffing model of this scale and industry was a significant investment for our mid-sized museum. Curatorial and education/visitor experience worked together to propose the budget and create the staffing numbers for exhibition cycles. In a fundamental way, the investment of curatorial ensured that the visitor experience was one of the important factors driving exhibition design, not the other way around.

The importance of various museum departments working together as a team and the product that can be achieved by designating a visitor advocate are evident in this practice. Kusuma says,

> Under the conventional museum education model, the gallery staff and the tour guides or docents are typically distinct from one another, each managed by a different colleague. This pretty much guarantees that there is a lack of synergy. I felt strongly that this had to change. The various groups needed to be brought together under one leadership, and each numbered more than thirty persons, to set about transforming the oppositional dynamic into the team- and visitor-focused Visitor Experience program. Curator-led and gallery educator trainings, which occurred at the start of new exhibitions, were held together; and guides and VA staff were regularly partnered for practice engagement. I established a new standard of collaboration and cooperation and stressed this collegial spirit in the hiring and training for both groups. As they did their tour planning, guides were often found in the galleries consulting visitor assistants about works, and visitor assistants were more actively and collegially supporting tours—especially large groups—through the galleries. A partnership was evolving, but it required consistent leadership and effort to maintain.

When asked how the success of the Visitor Experience program was measured, Kusuma answers,

> In all of the usual ways, formally and anecdotally, as well as a few others. Approximately three times a year, once for each major exhibition cycle, a third-party evaluator conducted extensive visitor surveys, measuring the museum on a variety of benchmarks. The gallery staff and guides were consistently rated above 8.5 (and often 9 or more) on a scale of 1 to 10. Anecdotal feedback included sentiments like these: "Excellent employees all around the museum"; "I was particularly impressed by how well-spoken and friendly the staff was"; and "You have really fantastic, friendly, knowledgeable staff in the exhibit halls. Everyone we interacted with was a pleasure." We received similar feedback across social media channels. Perhaps the best measure of success was the rate of adoption of our model by other museum organizations. Ours was a sought-

after model and we received dozens of requests for sharing information and resources. The Queens Museum, for example, created their Visitor Experience Agent program after visiting and studying the ICA's model.

Kusuma and ICA's prototype clearly illustrates the benefit that can be realized when the visitor experience staff within a museum is given the opportunity to curate the museum experience.

The Digital Technology Engagement Experience

To stay relevant to the millennial generation and younger, museums have learned to embrace technology. When the 2020 COVID-19 pandemic took the world by storm, for a time, the only way to interact with a museum was through its digital offerings, and there was still experience to be had, just a different type. A visitor to a museum's digital platform still walks away with a memory about that experience. In most scenarios, the digital piece enhances the experiences. But during the pandemic, it was the full experience.

Most major museums now use technology to enhance meaningful inter-actions with their collections and to expedite education. There might be a companion app to be used as a guide through the galleries; there are now artificial intelligences, augmented and virtual reality experiences, and social media–hosted conversations.

These technologically based connectors are designed to strengthen the bond between museum and visitor—to intensify that connection.

Another piece of technology that can be quite helpful with engagement strategy is your computer system. Not all point-of-sale systems are sophisti-cated enough, and not all museums can afford software that has the capabil-ity—but whatever point-of-sale system is used at your institution, find out if there is a tool within it to help you track visitor behavior, such as return visits, purchase history, and so on. Even birthdays or interests can be helpful. I have had experience with four different points-of-sale software systems, all used in a museum setting; all four could track visitor behavior—I just had to figure out where and how to access those mechanisms. If you find that your system does not currently track visitor behavior, reach out to the company; with enough feedback from system users, this tracking can sometimes be included in a periodic software update.

A Peek Behind the Curtain

As another means of enhancing the experience, the sense of peeking behind the scenes provides visitors with a way to see what they feel is "off-limits" to others.

This tactic is useful because it speaks to the visitor's sense of curiosity and adventure, though even this could be considered a performance art. Harvard Art Museums now include a glass-walled conservation lab where visitors can experience the staff's activities. The Art Institute of Chicago took the idea further: over five months, a conservator worked in one of the museum's sunlit galleries to restore French artist Francis Picabia's 1913 painting *Edtaonisl* in full view of the fascinated public.

It's just another way to engage that visitor, to enhance that experience. Engagement (and, by association, experience) is a thread that runs through every department of a museum. All efforts funnel into that, ultimately, engaged visitor.

The Role of Social Media

In "crowdsourced curating" experiences using social media, visitors don't just view the curators; they get to become them. Innovative programming includes opportunities for engagement by letting the public select works to display in an exhibit. Can you think of a better way to elicit your community's buy-in and allow access and experience for those who may not otherwise be able to have it?

At Seattle's Frye Art Museum, they used Facebook, Instagram, Twitter, and Pinterest to give access to its public collection of 232 works of European art in their #SocialMedium show. In two weeks, more than 17,000 votes were cast, and the crowdsourced favorite went on display, along with the names and comments of 4,468 participants. Talk about giving the people exactly what they want!

It must be recognized that any time an individual interacts with a brand/product/museum, even if only digitally, they are tangentially considered a "visitor" and, therefore, efforts must be made to create a good experience for all those interacting with it.

Connecting the Content

Admittedly, guest experience personnel don't usually have much influence over creating these engagement opportunities (though, they should) but frontline staff can recognize that these are excellent opportunities, be proud of them, brainstorm on other engagement activities using their insights, and enable existing engagement activities to be shared.

The experience portion of these engagement opportunities is to make sure your visitors know that they exist and know how to use them. You may have the most innovative museum in the world, but if your visitors aren't aware of these elements, don't feel they are accessible, or don't know how to use them, those innovations are doing your institution no benefit. The delivery of the engagement will serve to enhance participation. As visitor experience curators, our responsibilities are to serve our visitors with a menu of fun connection opportunities that are available within our museums.

Anytime something is delivered with a people-first attitude, it will provide a more exceptional experience than when something is delivered via a "ticket-taker," who points to where the restrooms are.

It is up to the frontline guest experience personnel of a museum not necessarily to foster engagement, but to ensure the engagement connection is taking place consistently and positively. Embrace the shift from "curator knows best" to "the people that interact with the visitors have valuable insight to contribute." Within a museum, we are all curators. Some curate the objects, and some curate the experience—but all positions are of equal importance to long-term sustainability. Of course, the pinnacle action of the highly engaged visitor is the moment they convert to a member and supply a more sustainable, direct revenue source for the museum. The value-seeking member (who joins because they plan to come back within the year) will not provide the sustainability of the affinity member (the member who joins because of their connection to the mission and the museum's people). True engagement offers the opportunity to build up that affinity network, and your museum's bottom line depends on it.

Notes

1. Popova, Maria. "Simone Weil on Attention and Grace." *Brain Pickings*, February 3, 2020. https://www.brainpickings.org/2015/08/19/simone-weil-attention-gravity-and-grace/.

2. Blackwell, Elliott. "Mary Oliver." Begin in Wonder (blog)May 31, 2018. https://begininwondersite.wordpress.com/tag/mary-oliver/.

3. Blackwell. "Mary Oliver."

4. Rodley, Ed. "Defining 'Engagement.'" *Thinking about Museums* (personal website) December 4, 2019. https://thinkingaboutmuseums.com/2019/12/04/defining-engagement/.

5. Anne, Bergeron, and Tuttle Beth. *Magnetic: The Art and Science of Engagement.* Arlington, VA: American Association of Museums Press, 2013.

6. Simon, Nina. "Participation Begins with Me." In *The Participatory Museum*, by Nina Simon, 33–78. Santa Cruz, CA: Museum 2.0, 2010.

7. Simon. "Participation Starts with Me," 52.

8. Mancoff, Debra N. "Active Engagement: Enhancing the Museum Experience." *Encyclopædia Britannica.*, July 31, 2015. https://www.britannica.com/topic/Active-Engagement-Enhancing-the-Museum-Experience-2034489.

8

Post-Disaster Museum Experience

MUSEUM EXPERIENCE is a fairly straightforward topic. Usually.
During the late winter of 2020, the COVID-19 pandemic took the world by surprise. No one knew how to handle such a large-scale and disastrous event. Every part of life was upended—financially, mentally, physically, and emotionally. The coronavirus pandemic forced museums to weigh difficult staffing and programming decisions while continuing to serve their communities and fulfill their missions.

According to estimates by the American Alliance of Museums, museums nationwide collectively lost at least $33 million daily due to COVID-19-related closures. As many as 30 percent—mostly those in small and rural communities—faced the possibility of never reopening.[1]

The Tampa Bay History Center (TBHC) was closed for eleven weeks in total. It was eleven weeks of uncertainty while all eyes watched the growing numbers of COVID-19-positive individuals in Florida. To "flatten the curve" and to do our part not to overwhelm the healthcare system, many businesses closed. Some never reopened but, thankfully, the History Center eventually did, with tight restrictions in place for both staff and visitors. The pre-COVID museum experience hardly resembled the "next normal," post-COVID, and there was no model to follow.

A comprehensive reevaluation of our service standards and the journey of the visit followed. At the very heart of customer service is treating someone warmly, with open arms and a welcoming demeanor, things that would undoubtedly become more difficult given the 6-feet-apart social distancing rule, masks covering up smiles, and drastic control of visitation volume. Usually, a large number of people in the galleries was a good thing!

Before COVID-19, touchless interactivity tools, contactless transactions, and social distancing had very little relevance to the guest experience. But now, they are the reality, and the show had to go on.

During the shutdown, it was easier to know what to do. Bring as much of the museum experience as possible to your constituents—meet them where they are. Most people weren't allowed to leave their homes, so there was an inherently sharp focus. Marketing departments everywhere switched from their traditional concentration of encouraging would-be in-person museum patrons to enticing them to "visit" digitally through lectures, member events, homeschool programming, and so on. Marketing departments pivoted, doing their best to meet visitors where they were during the lockdown. Frontline museum workers know well that the social and emotional aspects can also be a significant motivation for a visit, so there was a need to provide more than just the ability to virtually tour the galleries or attend a program via Zoom. For instance, History Colorado added an area to their website that asked their virtual visitors to share how the COVID-19 pandemic has changed their lives. They offered various ways to document their virtual visitors' trials and tribulations in the face of the crisis. They also offered a place to commemorate wins and positive memories,[2] hence emotionally supporting their virtual visitors and inherently adding value to their experience with the museum.

As restrictions gradually lifted from total lockdown, people started to venture out of their homes, but the trickle back was tenuous and filled with unknowns.

Post-disaster, the way we once served our communities and visitors has changed—forever, in some cases. In ways, the change has been good because it forced us to look at how we do things and fine-tune them. An excellent example of a museum whose hand was forced for the better is the California Academy of Sciences where Rebecca Albright, a coral biologist, was studying the mysteries of coral spawning in May of 2020. Albright identified the right conditions, including water temperature and lighting that re-create changing day length and the cycling of the Moon, to get the coral to reproduce in the lab. But when she learned that she couldn't be in the museum when a coral was due to spawn, she and her colleagues set up an infrared webcam. "We never set up a camera before because we didn't need to," Albright says.[3] The live streaming camera allowed them to view the awaited spawning. "If we had missed this, we would have had to wait a whole year," she explained. As a result, the corals accumulated 1.6 million followers on social media channels.

Museums learned they would have to proceed smartly, with agility and flexibility, and prioritizing safety and technology. And there was value-creation born from the crisis—COVID-19 allowed a lens to reevaluate and update the methodology of putting visitors and staff first. It forced a tangible application of doing so.

Research reveals a focus on four primary areas to meet a post-COVID-19 culture head-on.[4] As we go through these basic ideas, you might notice that they are mostly "duh" statements, and I sometimes wonder why it took a pandemic to remind me of these basics. We learned lessons that, six months prior, I might not have even known we needed to be taught, and while the reason was shattering, it was also enlightening.

We will drill down as follows and consider these ideas in a museum setting:

1. *Focus on care and concern.* Reach out, but with support, not marketing. The time for "selling" your visitors something is not during a closure or mid-pandemic. The aim is to ensure that your visitors know you care. It was an excellent reminder to sell less, support more. With visitor and staff safety at the highest priority point it has ever been, it's an ideal time to focalize on the goal of being a people-first institution.
2. *Meet your visitors where they are.* We need to bring our museums to our visitors to continue serving our mission and remind them, "Hey, we are here, don't forget about us," and distract them engagingly.
3. *Reimagine a post-COVID world.* Finances will be tighter and digital resources will be more in demand as the world determines if we will ever go back to being dependent on physical contact.
4. *Build agile capabilities for fluid times.* Tap social media, not surveys, for quick and more transparent guest reads. Solicit frontline employees for boots-on-the-ground insight. Pay attention to signs of failure and often reevaluate the way you are proceeding. Each day brings an opportunity to learn more, and although the post-COVID reality has been volatile at times, it has brought a much-needed reminder of the benefits of agility and flexibility.

Focus on Care and Concern

As someone who is naturally impatient, my first thought upon reopening was, "How can we make money?" So focused on numbers, I wanted visitors and was frustrated when we initially had multiple days of just a handful of guests. It took some reflection to recognize that I, personally, was neither making non-essential purchases at that point, nor was I going into public places unless necessary. Yet, I was expecting others to do the exact opposite of what I was doing.

But what I was continuing to do and had been doing the whole time, was keeping a mental record of who continued to reach out to me, the organizations by which I felt supported and who missed my visits and business—those places were where I vowed to return. The institutions that were managing to add value to my life even from afar were the ones I would continue to support.

I care about our visitors and members all the time, but something the COVID-19 pandemic taught me is that I need to show them that more often. And so, when the time did come to reopen, we put our people first. We did everything we could to make sure they knew that safety would be the priority on a visit, and to let them know how much we had missed them.

This reinforces a previous theme of being a people-first institution—when your visitors and your staff feel as though you are their most important asset, they will respond. And being people-first includes all of your people, not just visitors. It's safeguarding the health and well-being of staff, stakeholders, community partners, and so on, as well. You build up that support system as big as you possibly can because, in times like COVID-19, it's what will sustain you.

Visitors and staff alike will be eager to return to your institution, but they must feel safe and comfortable to start on the path back to pre-disaster behavior effectively. Colleen Fernandez, visitor services manager of the TBHC, recalls a memory of a post-crisis initiative:

Upon reopening to the public, on Saturdays in the early morning hours before the museum would typically open, we offered "'members-only" access, and a particularly memorable morning featured two elderly members, who thanked us profusely. They shared with me how after staying at home for months in quarantine, they felt as though they could safely visit the museum and not worry that there would be too many others visiting at the same time. I checked them in at the front desk, welcomed them back to the museum, and told them about all the safety measures we had taken to ensure their visit would be as safe as we could make it. They stayed for the morning with most of the museum to themselves and ended their visit with lunch at the café. They had long been supporting us with their membership, but that morning I felt like we were here to support them.

The TBHC is one of the smallest entities in the downtown setting in which it is located, so we turned to our county's school system, neighboring institutions, and other longtime community partners to help put forth a response plan that encompassed their expertise.

We collaborated with our community partners to ensure a timeline with which we were all comfortable regarding closure and reopening to set a tone of community unity. All cultural institutions in our immediate community reopened at approximately the same time—the zoo, the science center, the aquarium—we wanted to show our community that the cultural arts scene was coming back online and that we were doing it together.

Your mission and values underline the meaningful nature of your people, so this is all about going back to basics. Stay true to who you are as an organization, and putting your people first will come naturally. Take the CEO of restaurant chain Texas Roadhouse, Kent Taylor, who donated his 2020 salary and bonus, along with a substantial personal donation, to support restaurant employees facing unexpected financial costs.[5] Taylor notes: "I have always said we are a people-first company that just happens to serve steaks. Giving up my salary is the least I could do to show my commitment to that belief. This is my family."[6] Such a compassionate and empathetic approach to crisis will provide a return of dividends far greater than the initial investment. Imagine the number of dedicated employees that he has now cultivated. Twelve other top Texas Roadhouse executives followed Taylor's lead and volunteered to give portions of their compensation and bonuses to their frontline restaurant workers. Together they were able to fund a distribution to their frontline employee's bank accounts of almost $2 million.

Meeting Your Visitors Where They Are

Meeting your visitors where they are—when they are sitting at home—struck fear in my frontline heart. If visitors aren't physically coming into the museum, then where does that leave frontline employees? I learned that it puts us in a more important place than ever.

Disclaimer: This does not include the full closure of a museum, which most, possibly all institutions did experience at the height of the pandemic; instead, this is for a post-emergency time, such as when you are reopening and when everyone, both staff and visitors, is under immense external strain. At this point, visitors will be coming in, just less frequently. This renders the interactions that frontline staff have with the visitors even more critical.

Rebuilding your visitation from the ground up can be hard work. Take the first four or five guests that are willing to visit and make their experience feel safe and supportive. Those four or five people will tell the next four or five people, and the goal is to grow from there.

Meeting them where they are is not just literal, though; it's also figurative. There are unpredictable levels of comfort around varying levels of emergency and crisis. Whether it's a worldwide pandemic, devastating wildfires, a record-breaking hurricane or blizzard, economic crisis, political crisis, or societal crisis, all kinds of situations will affect visitor behavior. The way someone emerges from a crisis will vary by individual, and frontline staff should be prepared to be flexible and tailor their approach to each visitor. Still, overall actions should provide visitors with safety precautions that restore trust.

Contactless transactions and interactions can be a useful tool in meeting the museum visitors where they are. They can put the visitor at ease by allowing them to maintain their space bubble.

Reimagine the Post-COVID-19 World: The Aftershocks of the Crisis

I am unaware of one museum or cultural institution that emerged from the COVID-19 crisis unscathed. We all experienced unforeseen, forced economic cost cuts, and if you didn't, you were in the minority. These cuts inevitably affect the guest experience, no matter where within a museum they've been made. Still, the guest experience staff's responsibility is to shield the visitors from this and not allow the experience to suffer.

The aftershocks of COVID-19 will be felt for many years, both financially and mentally. When could another disaster strike? How can we financially prepare for something so tenuous? From a frontline perspective, you can make sure your visitors know you appreciate them now. You can build up your membership and take care of them during a closure or a stressful time for your community. You can adapt to their needs and requests and distract them or offer them ways to engage. Some museums, like the National Museum of Organized Crime and Law Enforcement, even used the opportunity to put a practical spin on pandemic response; the museum has its own speakeasy and, immediately following their reopening, they gave each visitor a complimentary bottle of ethanol hand sanitizer made in the on-site distillery.[7]

Museums have long been thought of as "safe spaces." It's one of our responsibilities as a community gathering place. Post-disaster, and even during, you have the opportunity to be that for your visitors. Sally Tallant, executive director of the Queens Museum, illustrates the visitor desire for that type of space and hopes that her museum can be a place of refuge for people. She is fulfilling this by instituting various programs, such as weekly conversations with homebound seniors about the institution's collection, a program for caregivers to learn about art, and several live-video artmaking sessions for recent immigrants who don't speak English. In a *New York Times* article, she says,

This is a time to consider museums as places of care. There is a need to develop porous cultural institutions that are open, inclusive, and empathetic as we recover from living through a prolonged period of isolation and loss.[8]

Tallant hits the nail on the head with her desire to be a sanctuary for her visitors. It will be the first place they visit, once they are able.

Build Agile Capabilities for Fluid Times

Connecting to your community and your visitors can be as easy as reframing (possibly even temporarily) the museum experience.

Dumbarton House, in Washington, DC, was the home of the first Register of the US Treasury, the national headquarters of the National Society of the Colonial Dames of America, and is a museum and historical site. It enjoys 1.2 acres of gardens and terraces located on the outskirts of DC's Georgetown neighborhood. Executive director Karen Daly didn't want to limit Dumbarton House to online outreach after COVID: "People do want virtual opportunities, but there is some exhaustion with screen time. It's important to look for things that are therapeutic and rejuvenating, something people can do as a family."[9]

Usually, the grounds and gardens are inaccessible to the public. But in the post-COVID days, they opened them to visitors looking to jog or walk, have picnics, and work using the free Wi-Fi. Due to the positive guest response, they plan to keep the gardens open. Even though the look and feel of what Dumbarton House has historically offered will have changed, a positive value-adding experience can still be had.

Utilizing social media as a means of data collection and evaluation in real-time gives you the capability to access your visitors' thoughts and feelings after their visits, very close to the times of those visits. What's more, social media is inexpensive. Using it as a means for primary source evaluation of how your post-crisis measures are stacking up, you have a very affordable yet accurate way to collect opinions.

Another tactic is to task your frontline guest experience staff with collecting their thoughts and ideas on how visitors are adhering to, and their comfort level with, the safety protocols for post-crisis that your museum has implemented. Paying attention to the successes and failures of what guests are seeking in a post-crisis experience will be vital to planning as you go. And in the fluid post-crisis world, being adaptable to your visitors' needs as they change and evolve will keep your organizations viable.

Correspondingly, have a written plan. We all have a disaster preparedness plan—it's an American Alliance of Museums core document and something no museum could function without. Add a section detailing steps to take in the event of a sustained, long-term closure, and include what's needed to reopen once you can, post-disaster, so that when it occurs, you'll be ready. In the McKinsey article aptly titled "The Restart,"[10] they call this "a detailed-relaunch map." The crisis has changed how many business leaders make decisions, underlining a need to define a reliable, phased framework for action in a highly volatile environment for the restart.

Set up a team or a plan-ahead committee that can focus on satisfying and continuously reevaluating the operating model and goals to ensure the museum's direction over the coming months. They can set short-term goals, and they can focus on meeting each goal and reporting to the more extensive staff and board about progress.

They Won't Forget You

Making a good experience is the culmination of your efforts. The addition of post-disaster limitations perhaps makes it a bit more difficult; however, even in a post-disaster scenario, we can still ensure that each visitor has the best visit possible.

I have found that, in the worst of times, people long to have these experiences. They are seeking a distraction, a learning experience, familiarity, support, and normalcy. Your institution can provide that to them when they need it most, and they won't forget that.

Notes

1. Voon, Claire. "How Three Very Different Museums Are Dealing with the COVID-19 Crisis." *Editorial* (blog), Artsy.net (online marketplace), April 20, 2020. https://www.artsy.net/article/artsy-editorial-three-museums-dealing-covid-19-crisis.

2. "COVID-19." *COVID-19*, History Colorado (website). Accessed October 20, 2020. https://www.historycolorado.org/covid-19.

3. Pennisi, Elizabeth. "Shuttered Natural History Museums Fight for Survival amid COVID-19 'Heartbreak.'" *Science*, June 1, 2020. https://www.sciencemag.org/news/2020/05/shuttered-natural-history-museums-fight-survival-amid-covid-19-heartbreak.

4. Diebner, Rachel, Elizabeth Silliman, Kelly Ungerman, and Maxence Vancauwenberghe. "Adapting Customer Experience in the Time of Coronavirus." *Marketing & Sales*, McKinsey & Company (website), April 20, 2020. https://www.mckinsey.com/

business-functions/marketing-and-sales/our-insights/adapting-customer-experience
-in-the-time-of-coronavirus.

5. Haberman, Susan, and Rhonda Newman. "3 Ways to Stay True to Your Company's Soul in COVID-19 Crisis." *HR Daily Advisor*, May 14, 2020. https:// hrdailyadvisor.blr.com/2020/05/18/3-ways-to-stay-true-to-your-companys-soul -in-covid-19-crisis/.

6. Cawthon, Haley. "Following CEO's Lead, Texas Roadhouse Execs Voluntarily Give up Salary, Incentive Pay." bizjournals.com, April 10, 2020. https://www.bizjournals .com/louisville/news/2020/04/10/following-ceos-lead-texas-roadhouse-execs.html.

7. Baskas, Harriet. "State of the Art: How Museums Are Preparing to Open amid Coronavirus Crisis." *Coronavirus*, NBCNews.com, May 26, 2020. https://www.nbc news.com/business/consumer/state-art-how-museums-are-preparing-open-amid -coronavirus-crisis-n1213396.

8. Small, Zachary. "Museums Embrace Art Therapy Techniques for Unsettled Times." *New York Times*, June 15, 2020. https://www.nytimes.com/2020/06/15/arts/ design/art-therapy-museums-virus.html.

9. Collins, Mary Ellen. "Rising to the Challenge." *Community Engagement and Impact*, American Alliance of Museums (website), September 21, 2020. https://www .aam-us.org/2020/09/01/rising-to-the-challenge/?utm_source=American+Alliance +of+Museums.

10. Hatami, Homayoun, Sébastien Lacroix, and Jean-Christophe Mieszala. "The Restart." McKinsey & Company, May 5, 2020. https://www.mckinsey.com/business -functions/strategy-and-corporate-finance/our-insights/the-restart.

9

On Making the Museum Experience

A S YOUR GUESTS ARE LEAVING after a visit, how do they feel?
In this book, you have read about the people within museums. Museums have long been thought of as institutions that house objects, but that definition is changing, and the museum professionals on the front line can shape what it becomes.

The process of writing this book started shortly before the COVID-19 pandemic, and soon after the project began, the coronavirus struck. Museum resources were strained, institutions closed with no reopening dates in sight, strategic plans were rewritten, and leadership and department staff were left with more questions than answers. Many of our bright and enthusiastic colleagues struggled with their commitment to an unknown future. Hopefully, by the time of this book's publication, the COVID-19 pandemic will be fading in the rearview mirror; however, the ramifications, both personal and economic, will surely be felt for years to come.

The museum field is resilient and its people tireless; we will bounce back. When we do, as the American Alliance of Museum's *TrendsWatch 2020* report,[1] aptly titled "The Future of Financial Sustainability," supports, the essentiality of making every interaction—both at and with a museum—pleasant will be more critical than ever before. A positive experience will be what gets us through.

Post-pandemic, your museum may be facing any number of challenges, and they are very likely a magnified version of whatever issues your museum was facing pre-pandemic. As the world starts over, we can use this time to press the "reset" button and go back to basics with one of the difficult lessons the pandemic directly taught us—to put our people first. Lean on digital when needed to supplement, but no matter how far technology takes us, nothing will take the place of physical interaction.

During the interviews held throughout the process of this text, two main recurrent themes emerged. One, interviewed museum personnel agreed that they directly influenced their museum's success, and two, their dedication to experience trumped all other motivations.

The positive museum experience is not a product of what a museum thinks or says it does for its visitors, because the experience had with the museum, product, or brand speaks for itself. The organization does not dictate it; it is dictated by those people delivering the experience.

A museum that is neither focused on its staff and visitors, nor concentrated on fostering a culture of service, will not survive the bid for attention and resources in an age where there are so many demands on how one spends free time. Our purpose cannot be fulfilled by a stodgy, archaic approach in this digitally and technologically driven era.

Individuals involved in the guest experience can redefine what a museum does since museums are brought to life by their people; we are the magic of museums. The foundations of hospitality are the ingredients of that magic; kindness, accountability, encouragement, support, generosity, team, humility, and integrity. You'll notice these attributes are also the foundation of relationships. And these attributes are both philosophical and tactical. It's not a trickle-down effect; it's the firm foundation of a house that will support strong walls.

In museums, you rarely hear the words "gratitude" and "unity" mentioned when discussing technical topics. Accessioning and deaccessioning? Sure. Interpretation? Why not. Conservation? Of course!

But the people are why we are here. They are why we do what we do. It's easy to think that we are collecting things so that people can learn from them for years to come. We are informal learning institutions that present information to people, who then interpret it in a meaningful way for them. When you look at what museums do, they exist for their people—so developing interpersonal relationships is the only route to lasting impact.

Hospitality focused workers know the importance of empathy and tolerance; ten years waiting tables in college, and I learned not to take things personally, to be flexible, and to let things roll off my back. In my museum career, some of the most important traits I carry with me and use in my toolbox to be a good leader are things I learned as a restaurant server. The hospitality you show your visitors will create those memorable moments; it's what will bring them back, and it's what will sustain your museum.

To Begin

Take the self-assessment at the end of this text (appendix 1). See where you start and let it guide you in knowing what foundational areas of your experience need work. Invite others within your organization to take the self-assessment, along with your board and your volunteers. Be prepared to get candid feedback that may sting and not feel encouraging, but you must recognize your baseline to begin a growth pattern. And only by admitting which areas surrounding your guest experience need strengthening will you be able to focus your resources where they need to be concentrated candidly.

Then dig deep. Do self-exploration around what made a good experience that you found memorable. What was it about the experience? Did it make you laugh? Was it about watching the person you were with smile? Did you feel respected? Did you feel like you learned something? These experiences likely added to your life in some way. Share those feelings with others at your institution. This exercise will get them talking and thinking about how they can support making the museum experience.

When you and others at your museum can identify what about a museum's experience is vital to them, your organization will have found its motivation rooted in service, which is the heart and soul of a good museum experience. Embrace the changes that come; they may come at a price or be challenging to face, but the cost of not facing the necessary changes is far greater.

To take hold, the changes really can't be only adopted by you. To achieve results, you must collect the buy-in of your leadership, staff, board, volunteers, community, and stakeholders. Only then will the results last.

In Practice

Making the museum experience is an actionable project. It requires ongoing reevaluation to ensure the road you are heading down will get you to your intended destination. This is a good thing. When you continually reassess your needs, it will ensure the most current, changing matters are being addressed. We are all aware, especially post-pandemic, how quickly our circumstances can change.

In practice, making a museum experience is about investing in the people and the service culture. And it doesn't necessarily mean investing in a monetary way (which is good news because many of us don't have that kind of capital to expend), but rather spending time committed to achieving an environment of service and nurturing the cause. This behavior is not entirely free;

emotional work can be some of the most exhausting and time-consuming work that can be done, though it offers the greatest reward.

So, I urge you to start slowly, explain to those around you transparently why you think this is a necessary process, and take the self-assessment often. Every six months is a reasonable interval to assess where you are growing within your museum experience experiment.

You will find that the more you foster a culture of service, the more you will attract talent—staff, trustees, volunteers, all who represent your organization—who model the same behavior, rendering the process easier the longer it is in place. Putting it in practice means an overall shift in the values that your museum holds dear, and with one little spark (you) can instigate that shift.

Making the Museum Experience

Having reached this point in the book, you must love museums. The promise of wonder and magic that they hold, and their ability to let people be free and change communities, has a hypnotic effect.

Making a museum experience is passionate work. Colleagues who have been creating museum experiences for years were thrilled to share discussions about their triumphs and challenges. I was also reminded of why I work in the museum field by the experiences of those who make the experience. They provided great inspiration, and their willingness to share was humbling.

As for making a museum experience, the many individuals interviewed for this book, the case studies, and research studied all agree that if you show your visitors the kind of experience you want to have on a museum visit, their museum experience will be made.

Note

1. Merritt, Elizabeth, and Ashley Thompson (presenters of supplementary on-demand webinar). *TrendsWatch 2020: The Future of Financial Sustainability*, Arlington, VA: American Alliance of Museums Press, 2020.

Appendix

Making the Museum Experience

Self-Assessment

Score 4	I fully agree with the statement.
Score 3	I feel we mostly are in alignment with the statement.
Score 2	I feel we are progressing and developing regarding the statement.
Score 1	I feel we are struggling with some or all of the statement.
Score 0	This is not applicable at my museum.

1st - Use the Self-Assessment Rubric (above) to express your confidence in your museum's application of the Be Our Guest content.

Museum Experience
Self-Assessment

Museum Name:

Content Details	Score #
All employees of my museum know what museum experience is.	
I feel like we prioritize the museum experience in the Marketing department at my institution.	
I feel like we prioritize the museum experience in the Education department at my institution.	
I feel like we prioritize the museum experience in the Collections department at my institution.	
I feel like we prioritize the museum experience in the Curatorial department at my institution.	
I feel like we prioritize the museum experience in the Visitor Services department at my institution.	
I feel like we prioritize the museum experience in the Operations/Facilities department at my institution.	
I feel like we prioritize the museum experience on the Executive level at my institution.	
We have full board leadership support in prioritizing the visitor experience.	
We have a visitor experience mission statement that supports our overall mission statement.	
Our museum is as much an academic institution, as it is a community gathering place.	
I would describe the museum experience at my museum as "magical."	
Every department at our museum prioritizes the value of a positive experience.	
Our museum has a culture of service, to the visitors.	
Our museum has a culture of service, to one another.	
At our museum, front-line service personnel are viewed as a liaison between the visitor and the content.	

Our interdepartmental communication is excellent.	
I think our staff/visitors feel our museum is diverse.	
I think our staff/visitors feel our museum is equitable.	
I think our staff/visitors feel our museum is accessible.	
I think our staff/visitors feel our museum is inclusive.	
We have considered the Experience Economy and other for profit models when considering the operation of our museum.	
We have a business model in place, and our staff is aware of the model.	
Visitor to member conversion happens at the front desk. Membership acquisition is a major part of the visitor services philosophy.	
I feel all touch points with our brand are focused on a positive outcome.	
When a disaster or emergency hits, I feel our museum is well equipped to bounce back easily.	

2nd – Whether you feel confident or unsure about your understanding of the content, review your work habits and look for a connection. Enter a score from 1 to 4. 1 = never; 2 = sometimes; 3 = often; 4 = always

My Behavior	Score #
I prioritize the museum's experience.	
I work collaboratively with my peers.	
I listen to the ideas set forth by my peers, and feel that they know I value them.	
I know how to enact a culture of service.	
I feel like I know the front-line personnel at my museum, and I make efforts to make them feel appreciated.	

3rd – Consider how you honestly responded to your behaviors. How do you believe your behavior affects your success? Give yourself a point for responding!

_____
_____
_____
_____

125-91 = You and your museum value the museum experience, and your visitors! Excellent work. Please consider reaching out to a colleague at another museum and sharing your visitor experience prowess with them. We all benefit when we help others succeed.
90-50 = Share the text with others within your institution, anytime there is discussion around something; it pushes the agenda and gets wheels turning.
49 or below = Not to worry! This text is intended to help increase value perception of the visitor experience within your museums. Take the assessment now, implement the strategies that make sense for your institution and 6 months after implementation, take the assessment again. You are sure to experience a score increase.

Index

Page references for figures are italicized.

360° approach, 90
5 Great Things All Great Salespeople Do, 71

"A Conceptual Model of Service Quality and it's Implications for Future Research," 82
A Totally Inclusive Museum, 52
AAM. *See* American Alliance of Museums
access, 52, 69, 70, 82–83, 95–96, 98–99, 106, 109
accessibility, 4, 25, 43–44, 50, 51–53
Achor, Shawn, 73
actors, 58–61
ADA Compliance, 52
adaptive behavior, 11
Albright, Rebecca, 104
Amazon, 14–15, 56, 75
American Alliance of Museums (AAM), 2, 3, 44, 46, 51–53, 65, 79, 80, 103, 110
American Revolution, Museum of the, 33
Apartheid Museum, 92

apologizing, 15
appreciation, 19, 52
artificial intelligence, 11–12, 98
Art Institute of Chicago, 99
audience evaluation, 71
augmented reality, 98
authenticity, 39

Bailey-Bryant, Joy, 49
Baird, Mark, 35
Barrier, John, 16
barriers, 13, 50–51, 83, 95
benchmarking, 47, 97
Be Our Guest: Perfecting the Art of Customer Service, 13–14
Bergeron, Anne, 90
Berry, Leonard L., 82
Bezos, Jeff, 14–15
bias, 45, 48–49, 86;
    preset, 8;
    unconscious, 44–45, 48
Big Potential, 73
Boston Children's Museum, 69–71
Boston Consulting Group, 45, 48
brand, 1–2, 31, 57, 80, 99, 114
Burning Man, 75

Business Model Canvas, 67, *68*
Business Model Generation: A Handbook for Visionaries, Game Changers, and Challengers, 66
business, 14, 16–17, 22, 39, 46, 55–56, 59, 73, 75, 106;
    model, 65–68;
    of museums, 65;
    of people, 92

California Academy of Sciences, 104
"Can a Goldfish Show you How to Excite your Customers?", 75
Cantarera, Kyle, 32
Categories of Experience, 57;
    Educational, 57;
    Entertainment, 57;
    Escapist, 57;
    Esthetic, 57
Charthouse Learning, 59
Ciecko, Brendan, 68
clarity, 34
coach, 22, 48
cognitive computing, 11
Cole, Johnetta Betsch, 46
collaboration, 24, 26, 97
common shared humanity, 44, 47
communication, 22–23, 30, 33–36, 50, 82, 94
community, 2–3, 5, 8, 10, 14, 26, 31, 50–52, 56, 75–76, 80–81, 85–86, 89, 91, 94, 99, 106–109, 115;
    gathering place, 43, 44
competence, 82
concierge:
    experience, 13;
    service, 16, 72
connectors, 31, 60, 98
content creation, 31, 39
Cooper Hewitt, Smithsonian Design Museum, 93, 94
Coronavirus, 103, 113
costuming, 61–62
courtesy, 10, 82
COVID-19, 5, 24, 35, 98–110

creativity, 11, 25, 49
credibility, 82
crowdsourced curating, 99
c-suite, 47
culture, 2, 18, 21, 25, 29, 30–31, 40, 47–48, 51, 70, 105, 114–116
Curator: A Museum Journal, 83
curator of experience, 19, 91
customization of approach, 10

Dallas Museum of Art (DMA), 69
Daly, Karen, 109
DEAI. *See* Diversity, Equity, Accessibility, and Inclusion
deBortoli, Silvio, 16
demographic trends, 16
digital platforms, 90
disability, 50–51
diversity, 4, 7, 20–21, 25, 43–44, 46–47, 49–50, 53, 96
Diversity, Equity, Accessibility, and Inclusion (DEAI), 43–53
DMA. *See* Dallas Museum of Art
Donnelly, Colleen, 69–71
Dove, 75
drama, 23
Dumbarton House, 109

eatertainment, 55
ego, 14–15
electrical current, 90
empathy, 11–12, 24, 34, 36, 39, 40, 45, 114
empowerment, 11, 20
energy, 37, 90
engagement, 4, 8, 18, 24–25, 33, 56, 60, 68, 70, 76, 89–91, 93–100;
entertailing, 55
enthusiasm, 37, 74
equality, 4, 44
ethnically diverse, 44
experience-based benefits, 86
Experience Economy, The, 8, 9, 14, 55, 57–59, 61
experience philosophy, 7, 10–11, 40, 43

experiencentric, 9, 13, 18, 23
experiential:
    initiatives, 57;
    products, 8

facilitators, 31, 91
Facing Change: Insights from the
    American Alliance of Museums'
    Diversity, Equity, Accessibility, and
    Inclusion Working Group, 44
feedback, 17, 30, 35, 49, 51, 69–71,
    96–98, 115
Fernandez, Colleen, 106
financial sustainability, 15, 38, 65–66,
    77, 79, 81, 87, 113
Fish!, 59
Five Star Visitor Experience
    program, 69–71
Forbes magazine, 12, 19–21, 30, 81
Ford Fiesta, 76
Four Realms of an Experience, *58*
"Four Things I Learned When I
    Started Thinking About Museum
    Accessibility," 51
framework, 10, 38–40, 67, 95, 110
friend, 60, 69, 79, 81
Frye Art Museum, 99
funding mechanisms, 67
fundraising, 67, 79

GDP, 46
gender-diverse, 44
gender-neutral, 48
Gilmore, James G., 8, *9*, 55, *56*, *58*
Gravity and Grace, 89
Grounds for Sculpture, 35

Harvard:
    Art Museums, 99;
    Business Review, 17, 71;
    Implicit Association Test, 45
hedonism, 75
Helmstetter, Cynthia, 33
high-functioning team, *40*
Hill, Kathryn, 29

History Colorado, 104
Horowitz, Alexandra, 89
hospitality, 9, 32, 114
hubris, 38
HuffPost, 34
human interaction, 7, 11
hybrid roles, 18, 95

I Can Get It for You Wholesale, 61
ICA. *See* Institute of Contemporary Art
immersion, 57, 93
impressions, 59, 61
inclusion, 4, 25, 43–44, 46-48, 51, 53;
    plan, 47
inclusive, 25, 44, 46–50, 52, 62, 80, 86,
    94–95, 109
ingenuity, 2, 25
inquiry-based experience, 93
Institute of Contemporary Art / Boston
    (ICA), 94
integrity, 25, 114
intention, 47–49, 51, 62, 89, 92
interdepartmental communication,
    33–36
Interflora, 75
internal locus of control, 71, 74

Kohll, Alan, 30
Kusuma, Krista Dahl, 94–98

Lau, Jennifer, 38, 39, *40*
LGBTQ, 45, 48
Lott, Laura, 65–66

magic, 7, 13–14, 62, 114, 116
*Magnetic: The Art and Science of
    Engagement*, 18, 90
marketing, 2–3, 14–15, 18, 33, 56, 79, 81,
    87, 92, 103–104
McKinsey & Company, 21, 75, 110;
    Foundation, 44
membership:
    acquisition, 80, 84;
    program, 80, 85–86
memorabilia, 57

merging membership and visitor
services, 79–80
meritocracy, 71
Microsoft:
chief executive, 36–37;
Teams, 35–36
millennial generation, 90, 98
minority employees, disadvantaged, *45*,
48
mission, 4, 14–15, 20, 23–25, 29–31, 43–
44, 66–67, 86, 91, 100, 103, 105, 107;
statement, 9, 10
Mt. Cuba Center, 32
Museoprenuer, 68
museum as theater, 14, 58–59
Museum Board Leadership report, 46

Nadella, Satya, 36
National Awareness, Attitudes, and
Usage study, 85
National Museum of Crime and Law
Enforcement, 108
National Society of the Colonial Dames
of America, 109
neurology, 90
New Gold Standard, The, 10, 18
New Museum, The, 68
New York City Department of Cultural
Affairs, 49
non-experience-based benefits, 86
North Star of customer service, *38*

observations, 31
Oliver, Mary, 89
"Onetime Visitors to Lifelong
Friends," 3, 79
organizational chart, 20, 38
Osterwalder, Alexander, *68*
ownership, 39, *40*, 71, 76, 81
Oxford Economics, 46

Parasuraman, A., 82, *83*
participation, 48, 57, 69, 75, 89, 90–91,
100;
active, 92

Participatory Museum, The, 90
performance, 14, 21, 58, 60–62, 82–85
performance-based scheduling, 80, 85
personal observation, 8
philanthropic giving, 46
Picabia, Francis, 99
Pike Place Fish Market, 59
Pine, Joseph B., 8, *9*, 55, *56*, *58*
pipeline of giving, 79, 86–87
point-of-sale system, 98
positivity, 30, 31
professional development, 24
Progression of Economic Value, *56*
psychology, 90
purpose, 8, 30, 51–52, 62, 84, 91, 114

quadrants of customer service
delivery, *12*
quantifiable criteria, 49
Queens Museum, 98, 108

Rand, Judy, 83
recognition, 11, 15, 19–20, 23, 38
recovery, 17
recruitment, 20, 22, 25, 49
relationship brokers, 91
reliability, 82
resentment, 35
responsiveness, 82

Saglio, Ryan, 51
sales, 2, 22, 38, 59, 71–72, 75, 77, 79–80,
84–85;
training and tracking, 80;
people, 71–73
security, 2, 15, 18–19, 55, 62, 65, 82,
91, 95
self-assessment, 115–117
service, 2, 10–14, 18, 21–23, 25-26, 33,
43, 51, 69, 70–73, 75, 82, 90, 95–96,
103, 115;
culture, 29, 114, 116;
recovery, 15–17
Service Quality Model, 82, *83*
Service Stars, 31

shared ownership, *39*
Shermann, Cecile, 52
shoppertainment, 55
Simon, Nina, 91
stagers, 14, 31, 59–60
staging, 14, 58, 60
Streisand, Barbra, 61
Stubhub.com, 38–39
sustainability, 15, 30, 38, 46–47, 65–66, 77, 79, 81, 87, 100, 113

Tallant, Sally, 108–109
Tampa Bay History Center (TBHC), 79, 80, 84, 86, 79, 103, 106
tangibles, 82
Taylor, Kent, 107
TBHC. *See* Tampa Bay History Center.
team-building, 18
Ten determinants of service quality, 82
Texas Roadhouse, 107
themes, 24, 55, 61, 66, 69, 114
Trendswatch 2020, The Future of Financial Sustainability (AAM), 113
Tuttle, Beth, 90

US News and World Report, 18;
  underrepresented groups, 45, 48
understanding, 7, 33–34, 39, 51, 56, 69, 82
unified approach, 39, *40*
unique connections, 55

Van Gogh Museum, 67
VEAs. *See* Visitor Engagement Associates
VEX. *See* Visitor Experience Group
virtual reality, 11, 98
vision, 59, 91, 94
visitor:
  point-of-view, 82, 83;
  to-member conversion, 4, 80
Visitor Assistants (VAs), 95–97
Visitor Engagement Associates (VEAs), 33
Visitor Experience Group (VEX), 24–25, 32-33, 35, 92, 94
Visitor Experience Program at ICA, 94–98
Visitors' Bill of Rights, 83

Weil, Simone, 89
Wells Fargo Museums, 92
wellness, 31
We're Not That Hard to Find: Hiring Diverse Museum Staff, 49
Wittwer, Patrick, 92, 93
women, 45, 48, 75
Wong, Danny, 34
work altruists, 73
work isolators, 73
World Economic Forum, 56

Zeithaml, Valarie A., 82, *83*
Zoom, 36, 104

About the Author

Andrea Gallagher Nalls is the director of experience and operations at the Tampa Bay History Center, where she has worked since 2009, and is also the site administrator of Chinsegut Hill Historic Site in Brooksville, Florida.

She has published and presented nationally on various topics including museum membership, guest experience, and visitor services. Her passion is the application of service methodology to achieve a successful museum visit.

Andrea completed a fellowship at the Smithsonian Institution in Washington, DC, where she fulfilled a research project on creating positive museum experience, and she is an American Alliance of Museums peer reviewer for their Community & Audience Engagement Museum Assessment and Accreditation programs.

She has a BA in English and an MIS, with a concentration in museum studies, from the University of South Florida.

Andrea lives in Tampa, Florida, with her husband and two children.